The Survey Handbook
2nd edition

THE SURVEY KIT, Second Edition

Purposes: The purposes of this 10-volume Kit are to enable readers to prepare and conduct surveys and to help readers become better users of survey results. Surveys are conducted to collect information; surveyors ask questions of people on the telephone, face-to-face, and by mail. The questions can be about attitudes, beliefs, and behavior as well as socioeconomic and health status. To do a good survey, one must know how to plan and budget for all survey tasks, how to ask questions, how to design the survey (research) project, how to sample respondents, how to collect reliable and valid information, and how to analyze and report the results.

Users: The Kit is for students in undergraduate and graduate classes in the social and health sciences and for individuals in the public and private sectors who are responsible for conducting and using surveys. Its primary goal is to enable users to prepare surveys and collect data that are accurate and useful for primarily practical purposes. Sometimes, these practical purposes overlap with the objectives of scientific research, and so survey researchers will also find the Kit useful.

Format of the Kit: All books in the series contain instructional objectives, exercises and answers, examples of surveys in use and illustrations of survey questions, guidelines for action, checklists of dos and don'ts, and annotated references.

Volumes in The Survey Kit:

1. **The Survey Handbook, 2nd**
   Arlene Fink
2. **How to Ask Survey Questions, 2nd**
   Arlene Fink
3. **How to Conduct Self-Administered and Mail Surveys, 2nd**
   Linda B. Bourque and Eve P. Fielder
4. **How to Conduct Telephone Surveys, 2nd**
   Linda B. Bourque and Eve P. Fielder
5. **How to Conduct In-Person Interviews for Surveys, 2nd**
   Sabine Mertens Oishi
6. **How to Design Survey Studies, 2nd**
   Arlene Fink
7. **How to Sample in Surveys, 2nd**
   Arlene Fink
8. **How to Assess and Interpret Survey Psychometrics, 2nd**
   Mark S. Litwin
9. **How to Manage, Analyze, and Interpret Survey Data, 2nd**
   Arlene Fink
10. **How to Report on Surveys, 2nd**
    Arlene Fink

Arlene Fink

The Survey Handbook

2nd edition

THE SURVEY KIT
TSK 2

SAGE Publications
International Educational and Professional Publisher
Thousand Oaks ▪ London ▪ New Delhi

For information:

Sage Publications, Inc.
2455 Teller Road
Thousand Oaks, California 91320
E-mail: order@sagepub.com

Sage Publications Ltd.
6 Bonhill Street
London EC2A 4PU
United Kingdom

Sage Publications India Pvt. Ltd.
M-32 Market
Greater Kailash I
New Delhi 110 048 India

Printed in the United States of America

Library of Congress Cataloging-in-Publication Data

The survey kit.—2nd ed.
    p. cm.
Includes bibliographical references.
ISBN 0-7619-2510-4 (set : pbk.)
1. Social surveys. 2. Health surveys. I. Fink, Arlene.
HN29 .S724 2002
300'.723—dc21   2002012405

This book is printed on acid-free paper.

    05 10 9 8 7 6 5 4 3 2

Acquisitions Editor:	C. Deborah Laughton
Editorial Assistant:	Veronica Novak
Copy Editor:	Judy Selhorst
Production Editor:	Diane S. Foster
Typesetter:	Bramble Books
Proofreader:	Cheryl Rivard
Cover Designer:	Ravi Balasuriya
Production Designer:	Michelle Lee

Contents

Acknowledgments		ix
The Survey Handbook: Learning Objectives		x
1.	What Is a Survey? When Do You Use One?	1
	Survey Objectives:	
	Measuring Hoped-For Outcomes	6
	Where Do Survey Objectives Originate?	10
	Straightforward Questions and Responses	11
	Types of Questions	15
	Types of Responses	18
	Four Types of Survey Instruments	22
	Self-Administered Questionnaires	22
	Interviews	22
	Structured Record Reviews	23
	Structured Observations	23
2.	Sound Survey Design and Sampling	31
	Survey Design	31
	Experimental	32
	Descriptive or Observational	33
	Survey Sampling	33
	Eligibility Criteria	35
	Sampling Methods	36
	Probability Sampling	37
	Nonprobability Sampling	39
	Sample Size	41
	Response Rate	42
	Guidelines for Promoting Responses, Minimizing Response Bias, and Reducing Error	45

3. **Reliable and Valid Survey Instruments**   47
   Reliability   48
      Test-Retest Reliability   48
      Equivalence   49
      Internal Consistency or Homogeneity   49
      Inter- and Intrarater Reliability   50
   Validity   50
   Content   51
   Face   51
   Criterion   51
   Construct   52

4. **Appropriate Survey Analysis**   55
   Statistical Methods   55
   Independent and Dependent Variables   58
   Analysis of Qualitative Surveys   61
   Content Analysis of Qualitative Data   68

5. **Accurate Survey Reports**   79
   Lists   79
   Charts   79
   Tables   83

6. **Ethical Surveys**   89
   Ethical Principles for the Protection
      of Human Subjects   90
   Institutional Review Boards   90
   Informed Consent   91
      Purpose   91
      Contents of an Informed Consent Form   93
   Researcher Misconduct   94

7. **Reasonable Resources**   97
   What Needs to Be Done?   98
   Checklist of Typical Survey Tasks   98
   Getting Each Survey Task Done   101
      Identifying Survey Objectives   101
      Designing the Survey   103
      Preparing the Survey Instrument   104
      Getting Ready for the IRB   105
      Cognitive Pretesting of the Instrument   107

Pilot-Testing the Instrument 108
Questions to Ask When Pilot-Testing Survey
Instruments 109
Administering the Survey 112
Managing the Data 113
Analyzing the Data 114
Reporting the Results 115
Who Will Do It, and What Resources Are Needed?
Personnel, Time, and Money 115
Survey Tasks, Skills, and Resources 116
Time, Scope, and Quality 126
Survey Budgets 129
Costs of a Survey: A Checklist 130
Budget Justification 139
Guidelines for Reducing Survey Costs 140
How to Reduce Costs 140

Exercises 143
Answers 147

Suggested Readings 153
Glossary 159
About the Author 167

This book is dedicated to the ones I love:
John C. Beck, Astrid and Daniella

Acknowledgments

This Kit would not have existed without the help I received from the saints at Sage. For this book, I am thrilled to thank Ravi Balasuriya, Michelle Lee, and Janet Foulger for the cover designs of each volume as well as the great design of the slipcase. What would I do without Diane Foster? She helped make the first edition a reality, and did her magic again. Any errors that may remain are my fault and not hers. I also thank Larry Bramble, the typesetter; and, Judy Selhorst, the copy editor (who, like Diane, finds all those typos and corrected any inconsistencies between volumes). And, thanks, too, to Veronica Novak and Patricia Zeman for all their help.

I am truly indebted to my editor, C. Deborah Laughton, who is the best buddy and friend around. Not only is she the muse, but she is also the Godmother (to Astrid and Daniella). We have to keep writing so that we have her around. Thanks, C. Deb.

Lastly, I am deeply grateful to those who used the first edition of the Survey Kit for their suggestions for this second edition. In particular, I would like to thank the following people who provided reviews and helped make it an even better Kit for readers: Kathleen Sexton-Radek, Elmhurst College; Cameron Lee, Fuller Theological Seminary; Shanker Menon, University of Sarasota; Karen Evans Stout, University of Minnesota; Bonnie Rader, California State University-Long Beach; Juanita M. Firestone, University of Texas-San Antonio;Carol Lancaster, Medical University of South Carolina; Dan Johnson, University of North Carolina-Wilmington; David McCaffrey, University of Mississippi; William Lyons, University of Tennessee; Suzan Kucukarslan, Henry Ford Hospital; Alana Northrop, California State University-Fullerton; B.J. Moore, University of California-Bakersfield; and, Ashraf Ahmed, Morgan State University.

THE SURVEY HANDBOOK:
Learning Objectives

The major goal of this handbook is to introduce you to the skills and resources you need to conduct a survey. These skills include identifying specific survey objectives, designing studies and sampling respondents, developing reliable and valid survey instruments, administering surveys, managing data, and analyzing and reporting survey results. The handbook also aims to teach you how to organize survey projects and estimate their costs; it includes examples of management plans and budgets.

The specific objectives of this volume are as follows:

- Identify the characteristics of high-quality surveys

- Describe the usefulness for surveys of specific objectives, straightforward questions, sound research design, sound choice of population or sample, reliable and valid instruments, appropriate analysis, accurate reporting of results, and reasonable resources

- Distinguish among different types of survey instruments

- Define reliability and its characteristics

- Define validity and its characteristics

- Understand the characteristics and uses of qualitative surveys

- List the steps in a content analysis of qualitative data

- Interpret data from open-ended questions using qualitative methods

- Distinguish between figures and tables regarding their usefulness for displaying survey results
- Explain the ethical principles that should guide survey development
- Describe the main components of an informed consent form
- Describe the characteristics of survey researcher misconduct

1 What Is a Survey? When Do You Use One?

A **survey** is a system for collecting information from or about people to describe, compare, or explain their knowledge, attitudes, and behavior. The survey system is comprised of seven activities. These include setting objectives for information collection, designing the study, preparing a reliable and valid survey instrument, administering the survey, managing and analyzing survey data, and reporting the results. The survey system should operate in an ethical manner and have sufficient resources to achieve its objectives.

Surveyors can collect information directly, by asking people to answer questions, or indirectly, by reviewing written, oral, and visual records of people's thoughts and actions. Surveyors can also obtain data by observing people in natural or experimental settings.

Surveys are taken regarding political and consumer choices, use of health services, numbers of people in the labor force, and opinions on just about everything from aardvarks to zyzzyvas. Individuals, communities, schools, businesses, and researchers use surveys to find out about people by asking questions about feelings, motivations, plans, beliefs, and personal backgrounds. The questions in survey instruments are typically arranged into mailed or self-administered questionnaires (on paper or on computer, off-line or on the Internet) and into in-person (face-to-face) or telephone interviews.

Surveys are a prominent part of life in many major indus-trialized nations, particularly the United States. U.S. elec-tions are always accompanied by floods of polls. The U.S. Census is a survey. But although polling and collecting data on an entire population are two major types of surveys, they are very far from the only kinds. Type the word *survey* into any Internet search engine, and see how many listings you get. One recent search using a popular search engine pro-duced 3,260,000 listings. Among those were Web sites men-tioning surveys on art, travel, entertainment, business, finance, family life, health, and science. As Example 1.1 shows, surveys are used in widely diverse settings, from find-ing out about the social needs of new immigrants, to helping schools understand how widespread bullying is among ele-mentary students, to finding out about employees' home offices.

A surveyor's job can be very rewarding in its variety and in intellectual challenges. What does the typical survey expert need to know? One way to answer this question is to consider the requirements someone must meet to get a job as a surveyor. Example 1.2 is an excerpt from a typical adver-tisement for an employment opportunity that might appear in the classified advertisement section of a newspaper. The "duties" specified in the ad are the typical skills required to conduct surveys. This book introduces all of them: study design and sampling; survey instrument development, with emphasis on asking straightforward questions and develop-ing reliable and valid instruments (including in-person and telephone interviews and self-administered questionnaires); data collection; data management; statistical analysis and interpretation; and report preparation. This book also dis-cusses how to plan surveys and how to prepare budgets for them.

EXAMPLE 1.1
Five Surveys:
New Immigrants, Bullying in School, and Home Offices

Mail Survey of New Immigrants

How difficult is it to adjust to life in the United States? What are some of the social and health needs of new immigrants? How often do they return to their countries of origin? Schools, health centers, and social service agencies need to understand more fully the wide variety of concerns that may affect new immigrants. A survey was mailed to 2,000 South Asians living in all 50 states. Some of the questions included were as follows:

- What is your visa or citizenship status?
- In what country were you born?
- In what country was your father born?
- In what country was your mother born?
- What is your religion?
- What language do you speak most of the time?
- What language do you think in most of the time?
- How many times have you been back to visit your homeland since living in the United States?

Interview Survey on Bullying Among Elementary School Children

Face-to-face interviews were conducted with 500 schoolchildren in grades 3 and 6 to gather data that would help school officials to understand the extent of bullying in the schools. The following are some of the questions children were asked:

- How often over the past year have you told others that you would hurt them?

Example 1.1 continued

- How often over the past year have you slapped, punched, or hit someone *before* they hit you?
- How often over the past year have you slapped, hit, or punched someone *after* they hit you?
- How often over the past year have you beaten up someone?
- How often over the past year have you attacked or stabbed someone with a knife?

E-mail Survey of Home Office Workers

Nearly all businesses permit employees to work at home some of the time. Emu.com was interested in finding out how that company's employees organize their home work environments. Do they have access to separate dens or offices? What supplies do they have on hand? An e-mail survey was conducted to find out. The survey contained questions such as these:

- Do you have a separate room or space for your home office?
- Which of the following software is loaded on your computer?
- How often do you purchase office supplies?
- Which of the following is most likely to distract you during a working day?
- Which of the following is least likely to distract you during a working day?
- In a typical day working at home, how would you rate your productivity when compared to a typical day working at the office?

Survey of the Literature

A student in a doctoral program in education plans to write a proposal to prepare a high school curriculum

Example 1.1 continued

aiming to modify AIDS-related knowledge, beliefs, and self-efficacy related to AIDS preventive actions and involvement in AIDS risk behaviors. The student is told that the proposal will be accepted only if she conducts a survey of the literature that answers these questions:

1. What curricula are currently available? Are they meeting the current needs of high school students for AIDS education? Have they been formally evaluated, and, if so, are they effective? With whom?
2. What measures of knowledge, beliefs, self-efficacy, and behaviors related to AIDS are available? Are they reliable? Are they valid?

Observations of a City Council Meeting

The voting practices of a particular town's city council have come under fire. Voting is done by a show of hands, and many community observers have claimed that the counts are inaccurate because some people do not keep their hands up long enough for accurate counts to be made, and others, perhaps unsure of what is being asked of them, either vote twice or do not vote in recounts. To examine the nature and extent of the problem, researchers select two members of the community at random to observe 10 city council meetings. They are asked to observe and record information on the following:

- Which council members raise or lower their hands inappropriately
- How often inappropriate hand raising or lowering occurs
- The issues the city council is voting on when inappropriate hand raising or lowering occurs

EXAMPLE 1.2
A Job in a Survey Center

Project Manager

Assisting the department director in carrying out applied survey research, your duties will include formulating study designs and sampling frames; developing instruments; supervising data collection, entry, and manipulation; application of descriptive and inferential statistics; knowledge of qualitative methods; and interpreting results and preparing reports.

The best surveys have the following features:

- Specific objectives
- Straightforward questions
- Sound research design
- Sound choice of population or sample
- Reliable and valid survey instruments
- Appropriate management and analysis
- Accurate reporting of survey results
- Reasonable resources

Survey Objectives:
Measuring Hoped-For Outcomes

What should the survey ask? What information should it collect? You must know the survey's objectives to answer these questions. An objective is a statement of the survey's hoped-for outcomes. Example 1.3 contains three objectives for a survey of educational needs. A specific set of objectives like these suggests a survey that asks questions about the following:

EXAMPLE 1.3
Illustrative Objectives for a Survey of Educational Needs

1. Identify the most common needs for educational services
2. Compare needs of men and women
3. Determine the characteristics of people who benefit most from services

- **Objective 1:** Educational needs
  Sample survey question: Which of the following skills would you like to have?

- **Objective 2:** Gender
  Sample survey question: Are you male or female?

- **Objective 3, first part:** Characteristics of survey participants
  Sample survey questions: What is your occupation? What was your household income last year? How much television do you watch? How many books do you read in an average month?

- **Objective 3, second part:** Benefits
  Sample survey question: To what extent has this program helped you improve your job skills? (In this example, you can infer that one benefit is improvement in job skills.)

Suppose you then add to these objectives the two objectives shown in Example 1.4. If you add objectives to a survey, you may need to add questions to the instrument. To collect information to meet the new objectives shown in Example 1.4, for example, you need to ask about the following:

- Parents' age
- How parents manage their household

EXAMPLE 1.4
More Objectives for a Survey
of Educational Needs

4. Compare younger and older parents in their needs for education in managing a household and caring for a child
5. Determine the relationship between parents' education and method of disciplining children for mild, moderate, and severe infractions

- How parents care for their children
- Level of parents' education
- Methods for disciplining children for mild, moderate, and severe infractions

When planning a survey and its instrument, you need to define all potentially imprecise or ambiguous terms in the survey objectives. For the objectives shown in Examples 1.3 and 1.4, the imprecise terms are *needs, educational services, characteristics, benefit, younger* and *older, household management, child care, discipline methods,* and *mild, moderate,* and *severe infractions*. Why are these terms ambiguous? No standard definition exists for any of them. What are needs, for example, and of the very long list that you might create, which are so important that they should be included on the survey? What is discipline? In a later section, this chapter addresses how you can use focus groups and consensus panels to determine a survey's objectives and help define and clarify the meaning of those objectives.

Survey objectives can also be converted into questions or hypotheses to be researched through a change in sentence structure, as illustrated in Example 1.5 with Survey

EXAMPLE 1.5
Survey Objectives, Research Questions, and Hypotheses

Survey Objective 4

To compare younger and older parents in their needs to learn how to manage a household and care for a child

> *Survey Research Question:* How do younger and older parents compare in their needs to learn how to manage a household and care for a child?
>
> *Null Hypothesis:* No differences exist between younger and older parents in their needs to learn how to manage a household and care for a child.
>
> *Research Hypothesis:* Differences exist between younger and older parents in their needs to learn how to manage a household and care for a child, with younger parents having greater needs.

Survey Objective 5

To determine the relationship between parents' education and method of disciplining children for mild, moderate, and severe infractions

> *Survey Research Question:* What is the relationship between parents' education and method of disciplining children for mild, moderate, and severe infractions?
>
> *Null Hypothesis:* No relationship exists between parents' education and method of disciplining children for mild, moderate, and severe infractions.

Example 1.5 continued

Research Hypothesis: Parents with high school educations or greater are more likely than parents with only some high school or less to use verbal disciplinary methods for all types of infractions.

Objectives 4 and 5 from Example 1.4. If you achieve Survey Objective 4 or answer its associated question or properly test its associated hypothesis, you will provide data on younger and older parents' needs to learn to manage a household and care for a child. Similarly, with Survey Objective 5, you will provide data on the relationship between education and methods of discipline.

The difference between stating a survey's purpose as an objective and as a question is a relatively minor change in sentence form from statement to question. Hypothesis testing is a different matter, because it requires the rigorous application of the scientific method. You should state survey objectives as hypotheses only when you are sure that your research design and data quality justify your doing so.

> For more on hypothesis testing, see **How to Manage, Analyze, and Interpret Survey Data** (Volume 9 in this series).

WHERE DO SURVEY OBJECTIVES ORIGINATE?

The objectives of a survey can come from a defined need. For example, suppose a school district is concerned with finding out the causes of a measurable increase in smoking among students between 12 and 16 years of age. The district calls on the Survey Research Department to design and implement a survey of students. The objective of the survey—to find out why students smoke—is defined for the surveyors and is based on the school district's needs.

The objectives of a survey can also come from reviews of the literature (that is, all published and unpublished public reports on a topic) and other surveys. A systematic review of the literature will tell you what is currently known about a topic; using the available data, you can figure out where there are gaps that need to be filled.

The objectives of a survey can also come from experts. Experts are individuals who are knowledgeable about the survey; they may be people who will be affected by its outcomes or influential in implementing its findings. Experts can be surveyed by mail or telephone or brought together in meetings. Two types of meetings that surveyors sometimes use to help identify objectives, research questions, and research hypotheses are focus groups and consensus panels. Focus groups usually contain up to 10 people. In a focus group, a trained leader conducts a carefully planned discussion in a permissive atmosphere to obtain participants' opinions on a defined area of interest. Consensus panels may contain up to 14 people; such a panel should be led by a skilled leader in a highly structured setting. For example, consensus panel participants may be required to read documents and rate or rank preferences. Example 1.6 illustrates how the literature, focus groups, and consensus panels can be useful for helping surveyors to identify survey objectives.

Straightforward Questions and Responses

Because questions are the focus of many surveys, it is essential that surveyors learn how to ask questions effectively, both in writing and aloud. A straightforward question asks for information in an unambiguous way and extracts accurate and consistent information. Straightforward questions are purposeful and use correct grammar and syntax. Surveyors should use questions that call for one thought at a time and for which the answers are mutually exclusive.

EXAMPLE 1.6
Identifying Survey Objectives:
The Literature, Focus Groups,
and Consensus Panels

The Literature

The Institute for Family Life is evaluating its 5-year program to prevent unnecessary placement of children in foster care. The institute will survey all 105 families in its program to gain insight into their perspectives on program participation. The surveyors plan to adapt an existing survey from other programs with similar objectives. This will save them the costs of developing an entirely new survey. The survey team conducts a literature review to find out about the availability of programs and surveys. They search PsycINFO, a database maintained by the American Psychological Association, using these keywords: *family preservation; family preservation* and *at-risk populations; family preservation* and *family crisis; family preservation* and *protective services.* The surveyors find 315 potential sources of information. Members of the survey team review the titles and abstracts of all 315 sources and decide to restrict their final search for surveys to studies of programs that lasted 2 or more years. They also exclude from consideration studies that are described only in books or book chapters, policy statements, editorials, or essays. The team is left with 25 studies that meet the criteria. Team members carefully review these 25 studies and find 2 surveys that appear to be appropriate for their needs.

Focus Group

A 10-member group—5 students, 2 parents, and 3 teachers—was asked to help identify the objectives and

Example 1.6 continued

content of a survey on teenage smoking. The group met for 2 hours in a classroom at the Middle School. The group was told that the overall goal of the survey was to provide the school district with information on why children start smoking. What information should the survey collect? What types of questions should be on the survey to encourage children to provide honest, and not just acceptable, answers? The focus group recommended a survey that would have at least two major objectives:

1. Determine the effects of cigarette advertising on smoking behavior
2. Compare smoking behavior among children with and without family members who smoke

Consensus Panel

Researchers conducted a two-round consensus panel to help identify the objectives of a survey to find out why children start smoking. The panel consisted of 10 members with expertise in survey research and smoking behavior among children; they included health professionals, students, and teachers.

In the first round, panelists were provided with a list of potential survey objectives and asked to rate each on two dimensions: the objective's importance and the feasibility of obtaining honest answers to questions pertaining to the objective. The researchers analyzed the panel's ratings to identify objectives that were rated very important *and* definitely feasible. The following table shows a portion of the rating sheet.

In the second round of the consensus process, panelists met for a half day and discussed the ratings result-

Example 1.6 continued

	Importance					Feasibility				
Survey Objective	Scale: 5 = Very important; 3 = Somewhat important; 1 = Very unimportant (circle *one* choice for each objective)					Scale: 5 = Definitely feasible; 3 = Somewhat feasible; 1 = Definitely not feasible (circle *one* choice for each objective)				
To determine the effects of cigarette advertising on smoking behavior	5	4	3	2	1	5	4	3	2	1
To compare smoking behavior among children with and without family members who smoke	5	4	3	2	1	5	4	3	2	1

ing from the first round. After their discussion, the panelists rated the objectives a second time. The researchers selected objectives for their survey that at least 8 of the 10 panelists had agreed were very important and also definitely feasible.

TYPES OF QUESTIONS

Purposeful questions. A question is purposeful when the respondent (that is, the person answering the questions on a survey instrument) can readily identify the relationship between the intention of the question and the objectives of the survey. Sometimes, the survey instrument writer has to spell out the connection between the question and the survey, as illustrated in Example 1.7.

EXAMPLE 1.7
Purposeful Questions:
The Relationship Between the Question
and the Survey's Objective

Survey Objective: To find out about reading habits in the community
Survey Question: In what year were you born?
Comment: The relationship between the question and the objective is far from clear.

The surveyor should place a statement just before the question that will clarify the relationship between the question and the survey objective. For example: "In this survey of reading habits, we want to be able to compare readers of different ages and backgrounds so that we can better meet the needs of each. The next five questions are about age, education, and living arrangements."

Concrete questions. A concrete question is precise and unambiguous. Adding a dimension of time and defining words can help to concretize a question, as shown in Example 1.8.

Complete sentences. A complete sentence contains a noun and a verb and expresses an entire thought (see Example 1.9).

EXAMPLE 1.8
Concrete Questions

Less Concrete: How would you describe your mood?

More Concrete: In the past 3 weeks, would you say you were generally happy or generally unhappy?

Comment: Adding a time period (3 weeks) and defining mood (generally happy or generally unhappy) add precision to the question.

EXAMPLE 1.9
Complete Sentences

Poor: Place of birth?

Comment: Place of birth means different things to different people. When asked for place of birth, I might give the name of the city in which I was born, whereas you might give the name of the hospital in which you were born.

Better: Name the city and state in which you were born.

When you create a survey instrument, you should make sure that experts and a sample of potential respondents review all of your questions. You should do this even if you are using a survey that someone else has used successfully, because your respondents may differ from those who have taken the survey previously in reading level or in interests.

Open and closed questions. Questions can take two primary forms. When they require respondents to use their own words, they are called **open**. Questions for which the answers or responses are preselected for the respondent are termed **closed**. Both types of questions have advantages and limitations.

Open questions are useful when the intricacies of an issue are still unknown; they allow for unanticipated answers and they let respondents describe the world as they see it, rather than as the questioner does. Also, some respondents prefer to state their views in their own words and may resent having to choose from among preselected answers. Sometimes, when left to their own devices, respondents provide quotable material. The disadvantage of using open questions is that, unless you are a trained anthropologist or qualitative researcher, you may find responses to open questions to be difficult to compare and interpret.

The use of open questions results in answers that must be cataloged and interpreted. Consider the question and possible answers shown in Example 1.10. Does 10% of the time (Answer 2) mean not often (Answer 1)? How does Answer 3 compare with the other two?

EXAMPLE 1.10
Three Possible Answers to an Open Question

Question: How often during the past week were you bored?

Answer 1: Not often
Answer 2: About 10% of the time
Answer 3: Much less often than the month before

Some respondents prefer to answer closed questions because they are either unwilling or unable to express themselves while being surveyed. Closed questions are more difficult to write than open questions, however, because one must know the possible answers or response choices in advance. But the results lend themselves more readily to statistical analysis and interpretation, and this is particularly important in large surveys because of the number of responses and respondents. Also, because the respondent's expectations (or the surveyor's interpretations of them) are more clearly spelled out in closed questions, the answers have a better chance of being more reliable or consistent over time. Example 1.11 shows a closed question.

EXAMPLE 1.11
A Closed Question

How often during the past week were you bored?

Please Circle One

Always 1
Very often 2
Fairly often 3
Sometimes 4
Almost never 5
Never 6

TYPES OF RESPONSES

The answer choices given to respondents with closed questions may take three forms. The first is called *nominal* or *categorical* (these two terms are sometimes used interchangeably). **Categorical or nominal response choices** have no numerical or preferential values. For example, asking respondents if they are male or female (*or* female or male) requires them to "name" themselves as belonging to one of two categories: male or female.

The second form of response choice is called *ordinal*. When respondents are asked to rate or order a list of items—

say, from very positive to very negative—they are given **ordinal response choices**. The third form of response choice, **numerical**, involves numbers, such as when respondents are asked about age (e.g., number of years) or height (e.g., number of meters).

Nominal, ordinal, and numerical response choices are illustrated in Example 1.12. Each of the questions in Example 1.12 produces different information. The first question asks respondents to tell if they have seen each of six films. The second question asks the respondents to use a continuum to indicate how important each of the six films is to them. This continuum is divided into four points (along with a "no opinion/don't know" option). The third question asks respondents to specify the month, day, and year of their birth.

Survey questions typically use one of three measurement classifications, as illustrated by the three questions in Example 1.12. The first question in Example 1.12, for instance, asks respondents to tell whether or not they fit into one of two categories: saw this movie or did not see this movie. Data or measures like these have no natural numerical values, and they are called nominal or categorical (the names are placed into categories, such as yes or no). A hypothetical survey finding that uses nominal data can be reported in numbers or percentages, as follows:

> More than 75% of the respondents saw at least one movie or play on the list, but no one saw all six. Of 75 respondents, 46 (61.3%) indicated they had seen *Star Wars*, the most frequently seen movie.

The second measurement pattern, represented by the second question in Example 1.12, is called ordinal. Responses are made to fit on a continuum or scale that is ordered from positive (*very important*) to negative (*very unimportant*). The information from scales like this is called ordinal because an ordered set of answers results. Ordinal data, for example, consist of the numbers and percentages of people who select

EXAMPLE 1.12
Three Questions About Movies

1. *Nominal:* Which of these movies have you seen? Please circle yes or no for each choice. (The response choices are categorized as yes/no.)

	1. Yes	2. No
Gone With the Wind	1	2
Schindler's List	1	2
Casablanca	1	2
Chariots of Fire	1	2
Police Academy	1	2
Star Wars	1	2

2. *Ordinal:* How important has each of the following films been in helping form your image of modern life? Please use the following scale to make your ratings:

1 = Definitely unimportant

2 = Probably unimportant

3 = Probably important

4 = Definitely important

5 = No opinion/Don't know

Example 1.12 continued

	Please circle one for each film.				
Gone With the Wind	1	2	3	4	5
Schindler's List	1	2	3	4	5
Casablanca	1	2	3	4	5
Chariots of Fire	1	2	3	4	5
Police Academy	1	2	3	4	5
Star Wars	1	2	3	4	5

each point on a scale. In some cases, you may find it expedient to compute the average response: the average rating of importance across all respondents. Sample survey results might take a form like this:

Of 75 respondents completing this question, 43 (57.3%) rated each movie as definitely or probably important. The average ratings ranged from 3.7 for *Star Wars* to 2.0 for *Police Academy*.

Surveys often ask respondents for numerical data. In Example 1.12, respondents are asked for their birth dates. From these dates, the surveyor can calculate each respondent's age. Age is considered a numerical and continuous measure, starting with zero and ending with the age of the oldest person in the survey. When you have numerical data, you can perform many statistical operations. Typical survey findings might appear as follows:

> The average age of the respondents was 43 years. The oldest person was 79, and the youngest was 23. We found no relation between age and ratings of importance.

Four Types of Survey Instruments

Survey instruments take four forms: self-administered questionnaire, interview, structured record review, and structured observation.

SELF-ADMINISTERED QUESTIONNAIRES

A self-administered questionnaire consists of questions that individual respondents complete by themselves. Self-administered questionnaires can be mailed or completed "on site," say, on a computer or by hand in a classroom, waiting room, or office. As an example, consider a student who is given a printed form with 25 questions on it about future career plans. The student is told to complete the questionnaire at home and return it to the teacher on Friday. Other types of self-administered questionnaires include Web-based, e-mail, and computer-assisted surveys. A typical computer-assisted survey presents the questions and the choices on a screen, and the respondent uses the computer keyboard to answer questions (see Example 1.13).

INTERVIEWS

An interview requires at least two people: one to ask the questions (the interviewer) and one to respond (the interviewee). (Group interviews are possible.) Interviews can take place over the telephone, face-to-face, or through videoconferencing. An example of an interview is when a psychologist directly asks a client to describe his or her family background and the psychologist writes the answers on a specially prepared form.

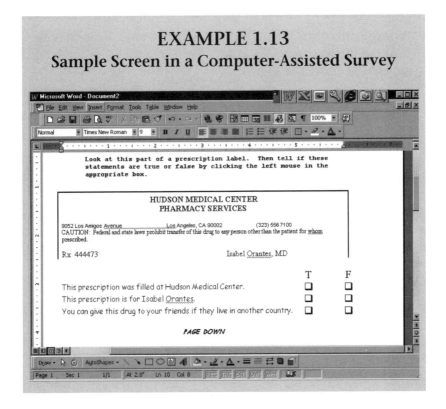

EXAMPLE 1.13
Sample Screen in a Computer-Assisted Survey

STRUCTURED RECORD REVIEWS

A **structured record review** is a survey in which the surveyor uses a specially created form to guide the collection of data from financial, medical, school, and other records, including electronic, written, and filmed documents. An example of a structured record review is the collection of information from school attendance records on the number and characteristics (e.g., age, reading level) of students who are absent 4 or more weeks each semester.

STRUCTURED OBSERVATIONS

In a **structured observation**, data are collected visually. Such surveys are designed to guide observers in focusing on

For more information on questions, see **How to Ask Survey Questions** (Volume 2 in this series). Objectives of that volume are as follows:

- Understand a survey's cultural, psychological, economic, and political context by doing the following:
  - Identifying specific purposes
  - Preparing appropriately worded, meaningful questions for participants
  - Clarifying research and other objectives
  - Determining a feasible number of questions
  - Standardizing the questioner
  - Standardizing the response choices

- Ask valid questions that
  - Make sense to the respondent
  - Are concrete
  - Use time periods that are related to the importance of the question
  - Use conventional language
  - Are appropriate in length
  - Use loaded words cautiously
  - Avoid biasing words
  - Avoid two-edgers
  - Avoid negative phrasing
  - Are appropriate in light of the characteristics and uses of closed and open questions
  - Distinguish among response formats that use nominal, ordinal, and numerical measurement
  - Are correctly prepared

- Correctly ask questions by doing the following:
  - Using response categories that are meaningfully grouped
  - Choosing appropriate types of response options

- Balancing all responses on scales
- Selecting neutral categories appropriately
- Determining how many points to include on rating scales
- Choosing appropriate placement for the positive and negative ends of scales
- Determining the proper use of skip patterns
- Apply special questioning techniques to survey behaviors, knowledge, attitudes, and demographics

- Describe the characteristics of focus group questions

- Identify the characteristics and uses of factorial questions

- Identify the characteristics and uses of conjoint analysis questions

- Understand the principles underlying questions in Internet surveys

specific actions or characteristics. For example, two visitors to a school would be participating in a structured observation if they are asked to count and record the number of computers they see, look for the presence or absence of air conditioning, and measure the square footage of various rooms.

For more information about self-administered and mail surveys, telephone surveys, and in-person surveys, see **How to Conduct Self-Administered and Mail Surveys, How to Conduct Telephone Surveys,** and **How to Conduct In-Person Interviews for Surveys** (Volumes 3, 4, and 5, respectively, in this series). Objectives of those volumes are as follows:

Volume 3, **How to Conduct Self-Administered and Mail Surveys**

- Describe the types of self-administered questionnaires
- Identify the advantages and disadvantages of the use of self-administered questionnaires
- Identify the advantages and disadvantages of the use of Internet-based questionnaires
- Decide whether a self-administered questionnaire is appropriate for your survey question
- Determine the content of the questionnaire
- Develop questions for a user-friendly questionnaire
- Pretest, pilot-test, and revise a questionnaire
- Format a user-friendly questionnaire
- Write advance letters and cover letters that motivate and increase response rates
- Write specifications that describe the reasons for and sources of the questions on the questionnaire and the methodology used in administering the study
- Describe how to develop and produce a sample, identify potential resources for a sample, organize the sample, determine sample size, and increase response rates
- Inventory materials and procedures involved in mail and self-administered surveys

- Describe follow-up procedures for nonrespondents, methods of tracking respondents, and number and timing of follow-up attempts
- Describe how returned questionnaires are processed, edited, and coded
- Describe data entry
- Describe how records are kept
- Estimate the costs of a self-administered or mail survey
- Estimate personnel needs for a self-administered or mail survey
- Fully document the development and administration of the questionnaire and the data collected with it

Volume 4, **How to Conduct Telephone Surveys**

- Describe the methods by which telephone surveys are administered
- Identify the advantages and disadvantages of the use of telephone surveys
- Decide whether a telephone survey is appropriate for your research objective
- Determine the method of telephone data collection to be employed
- Determine the content of the questionnaire
- Develop questions for a user-friendly questionnaire
- Pretest, pilot-test, and revise a questionnaire
- Format a user-friendly questionnaire
- Develop procedures to motivate participation and increase response rates
- Write interviewer specifications that describe the procedures used in conducting the interviews and collecting the data

- Write research or questionnaire specifications that describe the objectives of the survey, characteristics of the sample, and the reasons for and sources of the questions used in the telephone survey
- Describe the different kinds of samples used
- Decide on a sampling strategy and calculate response rates
- Describe how to develop and produce a sample, identify potential resources for a sample, and organize the sample
- Describe how to hire, train, and supervise interviewers
- Describe the need for and use of "callbacks" and "refusal conversions" and how to monitor them
- Monitor data collection and sample utilization to inform and improve data collection
- Describe the procedures by which completed telephone interviews become an analyzable, machine-readable data file
- Describe how records are kept and their uses
- Estimate the costs of a telephone survey
- Estimate the personnel needed for a telephone survey

Volume 5, How to Conduct In-Person Interviews for Surveys

- Describe the advantages and disadvantages of the use of in-person interviews compared with telephone and self-administered surveys
- Discuss the administrative considerations involved in setting up a project involving in-person interviews
- Write interview questions with structured interviewer instructions

- Distinguish programmer instructions from interviewer instructions for computer-assisted interviews
- Construct useful visual aids
- Organize a flowing interview script that considers possible question order effects
- Write an informative introductory statement
- Write a preletter
- Write a script for a precall
- Design an eligibility screen
- Write and appropriately place transition statements
- Understand the informed consent process and how to apply it
- Write a job description for an interviewer
- Develop an interviewer training manual
- Deal with interview refusal attempts
- Establish the environment for an in-person interview
- Record responses and correct errors in paper and computer-assisted interviews
- Design an interviewer training session
- Describe the role of a supervisor
- Understand the process of data cleaning
- Describe differences in quantitative and qualitative interview styles
- Describe cultural considerations involved in in-person interviews
- Understand issues related to the translation of interviews into other languages

2 Sound Survey Design and Sampling

Survey Design

A design is a way of arranging the environment in which a survey takes place. The environment consists of the individuals or groups of people, places, activities, or objects that are to be surveyed.

Some designs are relatively simple. A fairly uncomplicated survey might consist of a 10-minute interview on Wednesday with a group of 50 children to find out if they enjoyed a given film and, if so, why. Such a survey provides a description or portrait of one group's opinions at a particular time—a cross section of the group's opinions—and its design is called *cross-sectional*.

More complicated survey designs use environmental arrangements that are experiments, relying on two or more groups of participants or observations. When the views of randomly constituted groups of 50 children each are compared three times, for example, the survey design is called *experimental*. Definitions of the major survey designs follow.

EXPERIMENTAL

Experimental designs are characterized by the comparison of two or more groups, at least one of which is experimental and at least one of which is a control (or comparison) group. An experimental group is given a new or untested innovative program, intervention, or treatment. The control group is given an alternative (e.g., the traditional program or no program at all). A group is any collective unit. Sometimes, the unit is made up of individuals with a common experience, such as men who have had surgery, children who are in a reading program, or victims of violence. At other times, the unit is naturally occurring: a classroom, a business, or a hospital.

Concurrent controls in which participants are randomly assigned to groups. **Concurrent** means that the groups studied are assembled at the same time. For example, when 10 of 20 schools are randomly assigned to an experimental group and the other 10 are assigned to a control group at the same time, you have a randomized controlled trial or true experiment.

Concurrent controls in which participants are not randomly assigned to groups. When participants are not randomly assigned to groups, the groups are called nonequivalent controls, and the resulting studies are called nonrandomized controlled trials or quasi-experiments.

Self-controls. When one group is surveyed at two different times, it acts as its own control group. Studies using such **self-controls** require premeasures and postmeasures and are called longitudinal, pretest-posttest, or before-after designs.

Historical controls. Studies using **historical controls** make use of data collected from participants in other surveys.

Combinations. Survey designs can employ combinations of the elements noted above. For example, they can use concurrent controls with or without pre- and postmeasures.

DESCRIPTIVE OR OBSERVATIONAL

Descriptive designs (also called observational designs) produce information on groups and phenomena that already exist. No new groups are created.

Cross sections. Cross-sectional designs provide descriptive data at one fixed point in time. A survey of American voters' current choices is a **cross-sectional survey**.

Cohorts. **Cohort designs** are forward-looking, or prospective, designs that provide data about changes in specific populations. Suppose a survey of the aspirations of athletes who participated in the 1996 Olympic Games is conducted in 1996, 2000, and 2004. This is a cohort design; in this case, the cohort is 1996 Olympians.

Cohort designs can also be retrospective, or look back over time (a historical cohort) if the events being studied actually occurred before the onset of the survey. For example, suppose the members of a particular group were diagnosed 10 years ago with a certain disease. If you survey their medical records to the present time, you are using a retrospective cohort.

Case controls. Studies employing **case controls** are retrospective studies that go back in time to help explain current phenomena. At least two groups are included. When you survey the medical records of a sample of smokers and nonsmokers of the same age, health, and socioeconomic status and then compare the findings, you are using a case-control design.

Survey Sampling

A **sample** is a portion or subset of a larger group called a *population*. Surveys often use samples rather than populations. A good sample is a miniature version of the population of which it is a part—just like it, only smaller. The best sample is representative, or a model, of the population. A sample is

For more information on survey designs, see **How to Design Survey Studies** (Volume 6 in this series). Objectives of that volume are as follows:

- Describe the major features of high-quality survey systems

- Identify the questions that structure survey designs

- Distinguish between experimental and observational designs

- Explain the characteristics, benefits, and concerns of these designs:

    - Concurrent controls with random assignment

    - Concurrent controls without random assignment

    - Self-controls

    - Historical controls

    - Solomon four-group designs

    - Descriptive and experimental factorial designs

    - Cross-sectional designs

    - Cohort designs

    - Case-control designs

- Identify the risks to a design's internal validity

- Identify the risks to a design's external validity

representative of the population if important characteristics (e.g., age, gender, health status) are distributed similarly in both groups. Suppose the population of interest consists of 1,000 people, 50% of whom are male, with 45% over 65 years of age. A representative sample will have fewer people—say, 500—but will also consist of 50% males, with 45% over age 65.

No sample is perfect. Usually, samples have some degree of bias or error. To ensure that your sample has characteristics and a degree of representation that you can describe accurately, you must start with very specific and precise survey objectives. You must also have clear and definite eligibility criteria, apply sampling methods rigorously, justify the sample size, and have an adequate response rate.

ELIGIBILITY CRITERIA

The criteria for **inclusion** in a survey are the characteristics respondents must have to be eligible for participation in the survey; the exclusion criteria consist of characteristics that rule out certain people. You apply the inclusion and exclusion criteria to the target population. Once you remove from the target population all those who fail to meet the inclusion criteria and all those who succeed in meeting the exclusion criteria, you are left with a study population consisting of people who are eligible to participate.

Consider the illustrations in Example 2.1. The designers of the survey in this example set boundaries concerning who is and is not eligible to be a respondent. In so doing, they limit the generalizability of their findings. Why would researchers deliberately limit the applicability of their findings?

A major reason for setting eligibility criteria is that to do otherwise is simply not practical. Including everyone under age 10 and over age 16 in a survey of smokers requires additional resources for administering, analyzing, and interpreting data from large numbers of people. Also, very young and older teenage smokers may be different from those ages 10 to 16 in their needs and motivations for smoking. Setting inclusion and exclusion criteria is an efficient way to focus a survey on only those people from whom you are equipped to get the most accurate information or about whom you want to learn something.

EXAMPLE 2.1
Inclusion and Exclusion Criteria: Who Is Eligible?

Research Question: How effective is QUITNOW in helping smokers to stop smoking?

Target Population: Smokers

Inclusion Criteria:
- Between the ages of 10 and 16 years
- Smoke one or more cigarettes daily
- Have an alveolar breath carbon monoxide determination of more than eight parts per million

Exclusion Criterion: If any of the contraindications for the use of nicotine gum are applicable

Comment: The survey's results will apply only to the respondents who are eligible to participate. If a smoker is under 10 years of age or over 16, then the survey's findings may not apply to that person. Although the target population is smokers, the inclusion and exclusion criteria have defined their own world or study population of "people who smoke."

Sampling Methods

Sampling methods are usually divided into two types. The first, called **probability sampling**, provides a statistical basis for saying that a sample is representative of the study or target population.

In probability sampling, every member of the target population has a known, nonzero probability of being included in the sample. Probability sampling implies the use of random selection. Random sampling eliminates subjectivity in choosing a sample. It is a "fair" way of getting a sample.

The second type of sampling is **nonprobability sampling.** Nonprobability samples are chosen based on judgment regarding the characteristics of the target population and the needs of the survey. With nonprobability sampling, some members of the eligible target population have a chance of being chosen and others do not. By chance, the survey's findings may not be applicable to the target group at all.

PROBABILITY SAMPLING

Simple random sampling. In **simple random sampling**, every subject or unit has an equal chance of being selected. Members of the target population are selected one at a time and independently. Once they have been selected, they are not eligible for a second chance and are not returned to the pool of possible subjects. Because of this equality of opportunity, random samples are considered relatively unbiased. One typical way of selecting a simple random sample is to apply a table of random numbers or a computer-generated list of random numbers to a list of prospective participants.

The advantage of simple random sampling is that you can get an unbiased sample without much technical difficulty. Unfortunately, random sampling may not pick up all the elements of interest in a population. Suppose you are conducting a survey of patient satisfaction with health services. Consider also that you have evidence from a previous study that older and younger patients usually differ substantially in their levels of satisfaction. If you choose a simple random sample for your new survey, you might not pick up a large enough proportion of younger patients to detect any differences that matter in your particular survey. To be sure that you get adequate proportions of people with certain characteristics, you need stratified random sampling.

Stratified random sampling. A **stratified random sample** is one in which the population is divided into subgroups or "strata," and a random sample is then selected from each subgroup. For example, suppose you want to find out if a program to care for the health of homeless families is effective. You plan to survey a sample of 1,800 of the 3,000 family members who have participated in the program. You also intend to divide the family members into groups according to their general health status (as indicated by scores on a 32-item test) and age. Health status and age are the strata.

How do you decide on subgroups? Choices concerning the strata or subgroups are made based on available evidence that they are related to the outcome—in this case, care for health needs of homeless families. Justifications for the selection of the strata can come from the literature and expert opinion.

Stratified random sampling is more complicated than simple random sampling. The strata must be identified and justified, and using many subgroups can lead to large, unwieldy, and expensive surveys.

Systematic sampling. Suppose you have a list with the names of 3,000 customers, from which a sample of 500 is to be selected for a marketing survey. Dividing 3,000 by 500 yields 6. That means that 1 of every 6 persons will be in the sample. To sample from the list systematically, you need a random start, which you might obtain by tossing a die. Suppose a toss comes up with the number 5. This means you would select the 5th name on the list, then the 11th, 17th, 23rd, and so on, until you have selected 500 names.

To obtain a valid sample, you must start with a list of all eligible participants or members of the population. This is called the *sampling frame.* Systematic sampling should not be used if repetition is a natural component of the sampling frame. For example, if the frame is a list of names, systematic sampling can result in the loss of names that appear infrequently (e.g., names beginning with X). If the data are arranged by months and the interval is 12, the same months will be selected for each year. Infrequently appearing names and ordered data (January is always Month 1, and December is always Month 12) prevent each sampling unit (names or months) from having an equal chance of selection. If systematic sampling is used without the guarantee that all units have an equal chance of selection, the resultant sample will not be a probability sample. When the sampling frame has no inherently recurring order, or you can reorder the list or adjust the sampling intervals, systematic sampling resembles simple random sampling.

Cluster sampling. A **cluster** is a naturally occurring unit, such as a school, which has many classrooms, students, and teachers. Other clusters are universities, hospitals, metropolitan statistical areas (MSAs), cities, and states. In cluster sampling, the clusters are randomly selected, and all members of the selected cluster are included in the sample. For example, suppose that California's counties are trying out a new program to improve emergency care for critically ill and injured children. If you want to use cluster sampling, you can consider each county as a cluster and select and assign counties at random to the new emergency care program or to the traditional one. The programs in the selected counties would then be the focus of the survey.

Cluster sampling is used in large surveys. It differs from stratified sampling in that with cluster sampling, you start with a naturally occurring constituency. You then select from among the clusters and either survey all members of the selection or randomly select from among them. The resulting sample may not be representative of areas not covered by the cluster, and one cluster may not necessarily be representative of another.

NONPROBABILITY SAMPLING

Nonprobability sampling does not guarantee that all eligible units have an equal chance of being included in a sample. The main advantages of nonprobability samples are that they are relatively convenient and economical, and they are appropriate for use in many surveys. The main disadvantage of such samples is that they are vulnerable to selection biases. Two uses of nonprobability sampling are illustrated in Example 2.2.

EXAMPLE 2.2
Sample Reasons for Using
Nonprobability Samples

Surveys of Hard-to-Identify Groups

A survey of the goals and aspirations of members of teenage gangs is conducted. Known gang members are asked to suggest at least three others to be interviewed.

Comment: Implementing a probability sampling method among this population is not practical because of potential difficulties in obtaining cooperation from and completing interviews with all eligible respondents.

Surveys in Pilot Situations

A questionnaire is mailed to 35 nurses who participated in a workshop to learn about the use of a computer in treating nursing home patients with fever. The results of the survey will be used in deciding whether to sponsor a formal trial and evaluation of the workshop with other nurses.

Comment: The purpose of the survey is to decide whether to try out and evaluate the workshop formally. Because the data are to be used as a planning activity and not to disseminate or advocate the workshop, a nonprobability sampling method is appropriate.

The following are three commonly used nonprobability sampling methods:

- *Convenience sampling:* **A convenience sample** is a group of individuals who are ready and available. For example, a survey that relies on people in a shopping mall is using a convenience sample.
- *Snowball sampling:* **Snowball sampling** relies on previously identified members of a group to identify other members of the population. As newly identified members name others, the sample snowballs. This technique is used when a population listing is unavailable and cannot be compiled. For example, surveys of teenage gang members and illegal aliens might use snowball sampling because no membership lists are available for such groups.
- *Quota sampling:* **Quota sampling** divides the population being studied into subgroups, such as male and female or younger and older. The researcher then estimates the proportion of people in each subgroup (e.g., younger and older males and younger and older females).

Sample Size

The **size of the sample** refers to the number of units that must be surveyed in order for the study to result in precise and reliable findings. The units can be people (e.g., men and women over and under 45 years of age), places (e.g., counties, hospitals, schools), or things (e.g., medical or school records).

When you increase the sample size, you increase the survey's costs. Larger samples mean increased costs for data collection (especially for interviews), data processing, and analysis. Moreover, increasing the sample size may divert attention from other sampling activities, such as following up on eligible people who fail to respond, and so may actually increase total sampling error. It is very important to remember that many factors affect the amount of error or chance variation in the sample. Aside from nonresponse, these include the design of a sample. If the sample design deviates from simple random sampling, relies on cluster sampling, or does not use probability sampling, then the total error will invariably decrease the quality of the survey's findings. The size of the sample, although a leading contender in the sampling error arena, is just one of several factors you need to consider in coming up with a "good" sample.

The most appropriate way to produce the right sample size is to use statistical calculations. These can be relatively complex, depending on the needs of the survey. Some surveys have just one sample, and others have several. Like most survey activities, sample size considerations should be placed within a broad context.

Response Rate

All surveyors hope for high response rates. The **response rate** is the number of actual respondents (numerator) divided by the number of *eligible* respondents (denominator). No single response rate is considered standard. In some surveys, response rates of between 95% and 100% are expected; in others, 70% is considered adequate.

Consider the two surveys described in Example 2.3. The first survey uses past information to estimate the probable response rate. The survey oversamples in the hope that the desired number of respondents will participate. Oversampling can add costs to a survey, but it is often necessary.

In practically all surveys, information is lost because of nonresponse. Nonresponse may introduce error bias into a survey's results because of differences between respondents and others in motivation and other potentially important factors. It is very frustrating and costly to send out a mail survey only to find that half the addressees have moved. To estimate how much oversampling is necessary, you should

EXAMPLE 2.3
Two Surveys and Response Rates

1. According to statistical calculations, the Domestic Violence Commission needs a sample of 100 for its mailed survey. Based on the results of previous mailings, a refusal rate of 20% to 25% is anticipated. To allow for this possibility, 125 eligible people are sent a survey.

2. Employees at Uniting Airlines participate in interviews regarding their job satisfaction. A response rate of 100% is achieved with this sample.

anticipate the proportion of people who, although otherwise apparently eligible, may not turn up in the sample. For mail surveys, this can happen if the addresses are outdated and the mail is undeliverable. With telephone interviews, respondents may not be at home. Sometimes, people cannot be interviewed in person because they suddenly become ill.

Unsolicited surveys receive the lowest proportions of responses. A 20% response for a first mailing is not uncommon. With effort, response rates on such surveys can be elevated to 70% or even 80%. Some of the methods for increasing response rates include follow-up mailings, the use of graphically sophisticated surveys, and monetary and gift incentives such as pens, books, radios, music CDs, and videotapes.

Nonresponse to an entire survey introduces error or bias. Another type of nonresponse can also introduce bias: item nonresponse, which occurs when respondents or survey administrators do not complete all items on a survey form.

This type of bias occurs when respondents do not know the answers to certain questions or refuse to answer them because they believe them to be sensitive, embarrassing, or irrelevant. Interviewers may skip questions or fail to record answers. In some cases, answers are recorded but are later rejected because they appear to make no sense. This can happen if the respondent misreads a question or fails to record all the information called for. For example, respondents may leave out their year of birth and just record the month and day.

To promote responses, minimize response bias, and reduce survey error, use the following guidelines.

Guidelines for Promoting Responses, Minimizing Response Bias, and Reducing Error

- Use trained personnel. Set up a quality assurance system for monitoring quality and retraining.
- Identify a larger number of eligible respondents than you need in case you do not get the sample size you need. Be careful to pay attention to the costs.
- Use surveys only when you are fairly certain that respondents are interested in the topic.
- Keep survey responses confidential or anonymous.
- Send reminders to recipients of mailed surveys and make repeat phone calls to potential phone survey respondents.
- Provide gift or cash incentives (and keep in mind the ethical implications of what some people think of as "buying" respondents).
- Be realistic about the eligibility criteria. Anticipate the proportion of respondents who may not be able to participate because of survey circumstances (e.g., incorrect addresses) or by chance (e.g., they suddenly become ill).
- Check the survey's reading level to make sure it is appropriate for the sample.
- Hire professional translators, but validate translations with potential respondents.
- Follow up with nonrespondents.
- Make certain you have enough resources to perform all survey activities.

For more information on sampling, see **How to Sample in Surveys** (Volume 7 in this series). Objectives of that volume are as follows:

- Distinguish between target populations and samples
  - Identify research questions and survey objectives
  - Specify inclusion and exclusion criteria
- Choose the appropriate probability and nonprobability sampling methods
  - Simple random sampling
  - Stratified random sampling
  - Systematic sampling
  - Cluster sampling
  - Convenience sampling
  - Snowball sampling
  - Quota sampling
  - Focus groups
- Understand the logic in estimating standard errors
- Understand the logic in sample size determinations
- Understand the logic in determining sample size, so you have the power to detect a difference if one exists
- Understand the sources of error in sampling
- Calculate the response rate

3 Reliable and Valid Survey Instruments

A reliable survey instrument is consistent; a **valid** one is accurate. For example, an instrument is reliable if each time you use it (and assuming no intervention), you get the same information. Reliability, or the consistency of information gathered by a survey, can be seriously imperiled by poorly worded and imprecise questions and directions. If an instrument is unreliable, it is also invalid, because you cannot obtain accurate findings with inconsistent data. A valid survey instrument serves the purpose it is intended to serve and provides correct information. For example, if a survey's aim is to find out about mental health, the results should be consistent with other measures of mental health and inconsistent with measures of mental instability. A valid instrument is always reliable, too.

Reliability

A reliable survey instrument is one that is relatively free of "measurement error," in which individuals' obtained scores are different from their true scores, which can be obtained only from perfect measures. What causes measurement error? In some cases, it may result from the survey instrument itself—for example, when the instrument is difficult to understand or poorly administered. A self-administered questionnaire on the value of preventive health care, for instance, might produce unreliable results if understanding the questions requires a reading level that is higher than that of the teenage mothers who are to respond to it. If the reading level is on target but the directions are unclear, the measure will be unreliable. Of course, the surveyor could simplify the language and clarify the directions and still find measurement error. This is because measurement error can also come directly from the examinees. For example, if the teenage mothers who are asked to complete a questionnaire are especially anxious or fatigued, their obtained scores could differ from their true scores.

Four kinds of reliability are often discussed: stability, equivalence, homogeneity, and inter- and intrarater reliability.

TEST-RETEST RELIABILITY

A measure is reliable, or stable, if the correlation between scores from one time to another is high. Suppose a survey of students' attitudes was administered to the same group of students at School A in April and again in October. If the survey was reliable and no special program or intervention was introduced, then, on average, we would expect attitudes to remain the same. The major conceptual difficulty in establishing **test-retest reliability** is in determining how much time is permissible between the first and second administrations. If too much time elapses, external events might influence the responses at the time of the second administration; if too little time passes, the respondents may remember and simply repeat their answers from the first administration.

EQUIVALENCE

Equivalence, or **alternate-form reliability,** refers to the extent to which two items measure the same concepts at the same level of difficulty. Suppose students are asked a question about their views toward technology before participating in a new computer skills class and again 2 months after they complete the class. Unless the surveyor is certain that the items on the two surveys are equal, findings of more favorable views on technology after the second administration could reflect the survey's language level (for example) rather than actual improved views. Moreover, because this approach to reliability requires two administrations, a problem may arise concerning the appropriate interval between them.

When testing alternate-form reliability, a surveyor may administer the different forms at separate time points to the same population. Alternatively, if the sample is large enough, the surveyor can divide it in half and administer each alternate form to half the group. This technique, called the *split-halves method,* is generally accepted as being as good as administering the different forms to the same sample at different time points. When using the split-halves method, you must be sure to use random selection in dividing the sample in half.

INTERNAL CONSISTENCY OR HOMOGENEITY

A survey's **internal consistency,** or **homogeneity,** is the extent to which all the items or questions assess the same skill, characteristic, or quality. **Cronbach's coefficient** alpha, the average of all the correlations between each item and the total score, is often calculated to determine the extent of homogeneity. For example, suppose a surveyor creates a questionnaire to find out about students' satisfaction with Textbook A. An analysis of homogeneity will tell the extent to which all items on the questionnaire focus on satisfaction.

Some variables do not have only a single dimension. Student satisfaction, for example, may consist of satisfaction with school in general and satisfaction with one's own school in particular, with teachers, with classes, with extracurricular activities, and so on. If you are unsure of the number of dimensions expressed in an instrument, you can perform a factor analysis. This statistical procedure identifies "factors" or relationships among the items or questions.

INTER- AND INTRARATER RELIABILITY

Interrater reliability refers to the extent to which two or more individuals agree in their ratings of given items. Suppose two individuals were sent to a clinic to observe waiting times, the appearance of the waiting and examination rooms, and the general atmosphere. If the observers agreed perfectly on their ratings of all these items, then interrater reliability would be perfect. Surveyors can enhance interrater reliability by training data collectors, providing them with guidelines for recording their observations, monitoring the quality of the data collection over time to see that the collectors are not "burning out," and offering data collectors opportunities to discuss difficult issues or problems. Surveyors can also improve **intrarater reliability**, or single individuals' consistency of measurement, through training, monitoring, and continuous education.

Validity

Validity refers to the degree to which a survey instrument actually measures what it purports to measure. For example, a survey of student attitudes toward technological careers would provide an invalid measure if it asked only about the students' knowledge of the newest advances in space technology. Similarly, an attitude survey is not considered valid unless the surveyor can prove that the people identified, based on their survey responses, as having good attitudes are different in some observable way from the people identified as dissatisfied.

Four types of validity are often discussed: content, face, criterion, and construct.

CONTENT

Content validity refers to the extent to which a measure thoroughly and appropriately assesses the skills or characteristics it is intended to measure. For example, a surveyor who is interested in developing a measure of mental health must first define the concept ("What is mental health?" "How is health distinguished from disease?") and then write items that adequately contain all aspects of the definition. Because of the complexity of this task, surveyors often consult the literature for models or conceptual frameworks from which they can derive needed definitions. When surveyors are establishing content validity in their reports, it is not uncommon to see statements such as the following: "We used XYZ cognitive theory to select items on mental health, and we adapted the ABC role model paradigm for questions about social relations."

FACE

Face validity refers to how a measure appears on the surface: Does it seem to ask all the needed questions? Does it use the appropriate language and language level to do so? Face validity, unlike content validity, does not rely on established theory for support.

CRITERION

Criterion validity compares responses to future performance or to responses obtained from other, more well-established surveys. Criterion validity is made up two subcategories:

- *Predictive validity:* This is the extent to which a measure forecasts future performance. A graduate school entry examination that predicts who will do well in graduate school has predictive validity.

- *Concurrent validity:* This is demonstrated when two assessments agree or a new measure is compared favorably with one that is already considered valid. For example, to establish the **concurrent validity** of a new survey, the surveyor can either administer the new measure and a validated measure to the same group of respondents and compare the responses or administer the new instrument to the respondents and compare the responses to experts' judgments. Concurrent validity exists when there is a high correlation between the new survey and the criterion. Establishing concurrent validity is useful when you have created a new measure that you assert is somehow better (shorter, cheaper, and fairer) than existing measures.

CONSTRUCT

Construct validity is established experimentally to demonstrate that a survey distinguishes between people who do and do not have certain characteristics. For example, a surveyor who claims construct validity for a measure of satisfaction will have to prove in a scientific manner that satisfied respondents behave differently from dissatisfied respondents.

Construct validity is commonly established in at least two ways:

1. The surveyor hypothesizes that the new measure correlates with one or more measures of a similar characteristic (convergent validity) and does not correlate with measures of dissimilar characteristics (discriminant validity). For example, a surveyor who is validating a new quality-of-life survey might posit that it is highly correlated with another quality-of-life instru-

ment, a measure of functioning, and a measure of health status. At the same time, the surveyor would hypothesize that the new measure does not correlate with selected measures of social desirability (the tendency to answer questions so as to present oneself in a more positive light) and of hostility.

2. The surveyor hypothesizes that the new measure can distinguish one group from the other on some important variable. For example, a measure of compassion should be able to demonstrate that people who are high scorers are compassionate *and* that people who are low scorers are unfeeling. This requires translating a theory of compassionate behavior into measurable terms, identifying people who are compassionate and those who are unfeeling (according to the theory), and proving that the measure consistently and correctly distinguishes between the two groups.

For more information on reliability and validity, see **How to Assess and Interpret Survey Psychometrics** (Volume 8 in this series). Objectives of that volume are as follows:

- Select and apply reliability criteria, including the following:
  - Test-retest reliability
  - Alternate-form reliability
  - Internal consistency reliability
  - Interobserver reliability
  - Intraobserver reliability

- Select and apply validity criteria, including the following:
  - Content validity
  - Criterion validity
  - Construct validity

- Outline the fundamental principles of scaling and scoring

- Create and use a codebook for survey data

- Pilot-test new and established surveys

- Address cross-cultural issues in survey research

4 Appropriate Survey Analysis

Surveyors use statistical and qualitative methods to analyze survey findings. Statistics is the mathematics of organizing and interpreting numerical information.

Statistical Methods

The results of statistical analyses can take the form of descriptions, relationships, comparisons, and predictions, as shown in Example 4.1. In the first set of results in the example, the findings are tallied and reported as percentages. A tally, or **frequency count**, is a computation of how many people fit into a category (men or women, under or over 70 years of age, saw five or more movies last year or did not). Tallies and frequencies are expressed as numbers and percentages.

In the second set of results in Example 4.1, the findings are presented as averages ("on average," "the typical" movie-

EXAMPLE 4.1
Statistical Analysis and Survey Data

A survey is given to 160 people to find out about the numbers and types of movies they see. The survey is analyzed statistically to accomplish the following:

- Describe the backgrounds of the respondents

- Describe the responses to each of the questions

- Determine if a connection exists between the number of movies seen and the number of books read during the past year

- Compare the number of books read by men with the number read by women

- Find out if gender, education, or income is related to or predicts how frequently a person reads books

Illustrative results of the above goals of statistical analysis are as follows:

- *Describe respondents' backgrounds.* Of the survey's 160 respondents, 77 (48.1%) were men, with 72 of all respondents (45%) earning more than $50,000 per year and having at least 2 years of college. Of the 150 respondents answering the question, 32 (21.3%) stated that they always or nearly always attended movies to escape daily responsibilities.

- *Describe responses.* Respondents were asked how many movies they see in an average year, and if they prefer action or romance. On average, college graduates saw 10 or more movies, with a range of 2 to 25. The typical college graduate prefers action to romance.

Example 4.1 continued

- *Determine relationships between number of books read and movies seen.* Respondents were asked how many books they read in the past year. The number of books they read and the number of movies they saw were then compared. Respondents who read at least five books in the past year saw five or more movies.

- *Comparisons.* The percentages of men and women who saw five or more movies each year were compared, and no differences were found. On average, women's scores on the Value of Film Survey were statistically significantly higher and more positive than men's, but older men's scores were significantly higher than older women's.

- *Predicting frequency.* Education and income were found to be the best predictors of how frequently people go to the movies. Respondents with the most education and income, for example, saw the fewest movies.

goer). When you are interested in the center, such as the average, of a distribution of findings, you are concerned with measures of central tendency. Measures of dispersion, or spread, like the range, are often given along with measures of central tendency.

In the third set of results, the survey reports on the relationships between numbers of books read and movies seen. One way of estimating the relationship between two characteristics is through **correlation.**

In the fourth set of results, comparisons are made between men and women. The term **statistical significance** is used to show that the differences between men and women are statistically meaningful and not due to chance.

In the final set of results shown in Example 4.1, survey data are used to "predict" frequent moviegoing. In simple terms, *predicting* means answering a question such as "Of all the characteristics on which I have survey data (e.g., income, education, types of books read, types of movie seen), which one or ones are linked to frequent moviegoing? For instance, does income make a difference? Education? Income and education?"

What methods should you use to describe, summarize, compare, and predict? Before you can answer that question, you must answer four others:

1. Do the survey data come from nominal, ordinal, or numerical scales or measures?

2. How many independent and dependent variables are there?

3. What statistical methods are potentially appropriate?

4. Do the survey data fit the requirements of the methods?

Nominal, ordinal, and numerical measures have already been discussed; the next section deals with independent and dependent variables.

Independent and Dependent Variables

A **variable** is a measurable characteristic that varies in the population. For example, weight is a variable, and all persons weighing 55 kilograms have the same numerical weight. Satisfaction with a product is also a variable. To measure satisfaction, however, a surveyor must devise a numerical scale and establish rules for its interpretation. For example, in Survey A, product satisfaction is measured on a scale from 1 to 100, with 100 representing perfect satisfaction. In Survey B, however, satisfaction is measured according to a count of the number of repeat customers. The rule is that satisfaction is demonstrated when at least 15% of all customers reorder within a year.

The choice of method for analyzing survey data is always dependent on the type of data available (nominal, ordinal, or numerical) and on the number of variables involved. Some survey variables are termed **independent**, and some are termed **dependent**.

Independent variables are also called *explanatory* or *predictor* variables because they are used to explain or predict a response, outcome, or result—the dependent variable. You can identify the independent and dependent variables by studying the objectives and targets of a survey, as illustrated in Example 4.2.

EXAMPLE 4.2
Targets and Variables

Objective: To compare elementary school students in different grades regarding (a) opinions on the school's new science program and (b) attitudes toward school

Target: Boys and girls in grades 3 through 6 in five elementary schools

Independent Variables: Gender, grade level, school

Characteristics of Survey: To get gender, ask if male or female; ask students to write in grade level and name of school.

Type of Data: All nominal

Dependent Variables: Opinion of new science program and attitudes toward school

Characteristics of Survey: To get opinions on new science program, ask for ratings of like and dislike (e.g., from *like a lot* to *dislike a lot*); to learn about attitudes, use the Attitude Toward School Rating Scale.

Type of Data: Both ordinal

To choose an appropriate analysis method, you must begin by deciding on the purpose of the analysis. You then need to determine the number of independent and dependent variables and whether you have nominal, ordinal, or numerical data. When you have completed these activities, you can choose an analysis method. Example 4.3 shows how this works. In the example, the choice of analytic method is labeled "possible." The appropriateness of your choice of a statistical method depends on the extent to which you can meet the method's assumptions about the characteristics and quality of the data. In Example 4.3, too little information is given to help you decide on whether the assumptions are met.

When a survey uses statistical methods, it is called a *statistical* or *quantitative* survey. When a survey uses qualitative research methods, it is called a *qualitative* survey.

EXAMPLE 4.3
Choosing an Analysis Method

Survey Objective: To compare boys and girls in terms of whether they do or do not support their school's new dress code

Number of Independent Variables: One (gender)

Type of Data: Nominal (boys, girls)

Number of Dependent Variables: One (support dress code)

Type of Data: Nominal (support or do not support)

Possible Method of Analysis: Logistic regression, a statistical method used when the behavior of interest has a dichotomous (divided into two) outcome—support or do not support.

Analysis of Qualitative Surveys

Qualitative surveys collect information on the meanings that people attach to their experiences and on the ways they express themselves. Qualitative surveys provide data to answer questions like these: "What is X, and how do different people, communities, and cultures think and feel about X, and why?" Statistical surveys are sometimes contrasted with qualitative surveys. **Statistical surveys** provide information answering questions like these: "How many Xs are there?" "What is the average X, and how does it compare to the average Y?"

Suppose you are interested in finding out how often children in a particular elementary school purchase certain snack foods each school day. In a statistical survey, you might ask a question such as that shown in Example 4.4. The items (potato chips, pretzels, and so on) on lists like these usually come from surveyors' reviews of the literature and their own experience with the subject in question (in this case, children's food choices). Marketing studies, for instance, can provide you with information on sales of specific types of foods so that you can choose the ones most likely to be relevant to your survey. The response scale used in the example (*often, sometimes, never*) is one that is familiar to many people, so it makes sense to use one like it.

But suppose the literature does not address the population of children who interest you? The children in your survey may buy foods that are not on the list, but that are important to learn about. Interpretations of what *often, sometimes,* and *rarely* or *never* mean may differ from child to child and may also diverge from yours. Also, the children in your survey may have difficulty understanding questions with closed response choices. If you have concerns like these, then a statistical survey is probably not appropriate. Instead, a qualitative survey is warranted.

In a qualitative study, you might ask open-ended questions such as these: "If you ever buy food for yourself during the week, what kinds of food do you buy?" "When do you

EXAMPLE 4.4
Sample Statistical Survey Question

How often in the past 5 days did you buy each of the following foods?

Circle one choice.

Potato chips	Often	Sometimes	Never
Candy	Often	Sometimes	Never
Pretzels	Often	Sometimes	Never
Hot dogs	Often	Sometimes	Never
Hamburgers	Often	Sometimes	Never
French fries	Often	Sometimes	Never
Other, please describe:	Often	Sometimes	Never

buy these foods?" "If you ever buy food like this more than once a day, why do you do so?"

Qualitative surveys are useful when you cannot rely on your own previous experience and the literature to guide you in designing closed questions or when you want detailed information in the respondents' own words. Qualitative surveys are particularly suited to examining the feelings, opinions, and values of individuals and groups, and to surveying people who are unable or unwilling to complete statistical survey instruments. They are also useful when you have access only to small samples.

Example 4.5 lists some of the uses of qualitative surveys. Suppose you are interested in surveying low-income, non-English-speaking people in order to find out how to improve the quality of their mental health care. In a statistical survey, you would identify a large, preferably representative sample

(text continues on page 65)

EXAMPLE 4.5
Some Uses of Qualitative Surveys

- To explore the knowledge, feelings, opinions, and values of individuals and groups such as the following:
  - Experts in a particular field of knowledge
  - Individuals and groups of people who have experienced or shared similar personal or communal problems
- To find out about the feelings and behaviors of people who are unable to participate in traditional surveys; for example:
  - People who cannot read or cannot complete self-administered questionnaires for some other reason
  - Those who are seriously mentally ill
  - The very young or the terminally ill
- To learn about the feelings and behaviors of people who are not likely to complete traditional surveys; for example:
  - Street people
  - Substance abusers
  - Persons who participate in illegal or socially unacceptable activities
- To find out about the feelings, opinions, and values of small numbers of people; for example:
  - People who work for a particular company or hospital
  - People who attend a particular school

Example 4.5 continued

- To learn abut people in their natural environment in order to

  - Identify how much time they spend in certain activities

  - Find out what goes on during a typical day at work or at school

  - Study the dynamics of individuals and groups while they go about their daily activities

- To supplement traditional surveys or guide their development in order to

  - Find out which problems and questions are important and should be addressed by the present survey as well as future research and policy

  - Generate research questions and hypotheses

  - Add depth, meaning, and detail to statistical findings

  - Find out how persons think, feel, or behave when standardized measures are not yet available

- To collect data when traditional research methods may raise profound ethical questions; for example:

  - Studies in which randomization cannot take place because the intervention or treatment is extremely likely to be effective and so an alternative is not possible

  - Studies of persons with medical or learning disabilities who cannot sign informed consent forms

  - The very young or the frail elderly

of non-English-speaking people and survey them in the languages they speak. The survey instrument might be a self-administered questionnaire or an interview including questions such as those shown in Example 4.6.

EXAMPLE 4.6
Questions for a Survey About the Quality of Mental Health Care

During the *past 3 months,* did you take any prescribed medications for personal, mental, or emotional problems, such as depression, anxiety, nerves, or alcohol or drug abuse?

Yes ❑

No ❑

During the *past 3 months,* did you see any of the following for personal, mental, or emotional problems, such as depression, anxiety, nerves, or alcohol or drug abuse?

Priest ❑

Chiropractor ❑

Herbalist or naturalist ❑

Massage therapist or *sobrador* ❑

Witchcraft doctor or *curandero* ❑

In a qualitative survey on the same topic, you might go to local community mental health clinics and interview the clients in order to get in-depth information in their own words. What do they need and prefer regarding mental health care? What do they do when they are depressed or anxious? Example 4.7 shows how this approach might work.

EXAMPLE 4.7
A Qualitative Survey to Improve
Mental Health Care for Spanish-Speaking Adults

Many low-income, primarily Spanish-speaking people in this community use the Chavez Community Clinic for mental health services. Studies have shown that people in general adhere to recommended mental health treatments only if the regimens fit into their daily schedules. People who work during the day, like most of the adults at Chavez, have difficulty getting their employers to give them time off to attend recommended counseling sessions. What can be done about this? What alternative days and times for sessions are possible? Studies also show that people do best if their recommended treatments are culturally appropriate. How do people at Chavez define and explain their culture? Are cultural preferences and values being ignored? If so, what should be done? To answer questions like these, three groups of 10 people at Chavez are brought together and interviewed in Spanish. The interviewees are selected to represent consumers and their advocates. The interviewer uses a set of topics (rather than questions) to guide the discussion. The interviewer aims to promote an in-depth discussion.

Example 4.8 illustrates three other qualitative surveys in action. What do these survey scenarios have in common? Where do they differ? The surveys share two basic features:

- They rely on relatively small numbers of observations (9 films, 6 meetings, 24 students, 2 nursing homes).

- They take place in local settings (1 school, project, office, nursing home).

EXAMPLE 4.8
Qualitative Surveys in Action

Survey Objective: To identify the goals of teenage girls in an immigrant culture in a large U.S. city

Method: Review the content of nine short films made over a 3-year period. The American Film Society sponsored the films and all cover the filmmakers' goals and aspirations.

Survey Objective: To improve the efficiency of project monthly meetings

Method: Observe meetings over a 6-month period.

Survey Objective: To examine dating patterns among college students

Method: First, interview four groups of 6 students; then, interview each of the 24 students individually.

Survey Objective: To examine the typical routines of elderly residents in a retirement home

Method: Observe the daily activities of residents in a public nursing home and a private nursing home over a 3-month period.

Qualitative surveys are particularly useful when you don't have or want large numbers of people to participate. In fact, increases in sample size will increase the complexity of data collection, management, and analysis without necessarily improving the quality or credibility of the results. For instance, suppose you interview 30 or even 50 students, rather than 24 (as in Example 4.8), to find out about their dating patterns. Is the increase likely to improve your results? To answer this question properly, you need to design an experiment in which you compare the quality of the answers you receive from differing numbers of students. Without these data, you can base your answer only on your experience and judgment.

Researchers who employ qualitative surveys do not necessarily aim for representative or generalizable results, nor do they aspire to provide information on the "typical" or "average" individual. Their purpose in using qualitative surveys is to provide depth and individual meaning to the questions of interest. "Depth and uniqueness" rather than breadth and representation should be a qualitative survey motto.

Where do the surveys described in Example 4.8 differ? They differ in their sources of survey information: "text," observations, and interviews. Watching people in their own territory may mean reviewing texts (written, oral, visual) or observing and talking with people (interviews, focus groups, consensus panels). Example 4.9 shows the most common sources of information for qualitative surveys and how they are used.

Content Analysis of Qualitative Data

Content analysis is a method for analyzing and interpreting qualitative survey results. Qualitative results usually come from written or recorded documents and observations of behavior. The results of qualitative surveys are often characterized by vast amounts of information that must be summarized, analyzed, and interpreted.

The first step in a content analysis is to assemble the data and become extremely familiar with the subject matter of the transcripts, notes, and/or tapes. This may mean reading through hundreds of pages of recorded text, watching hours or days of film, listening to tapes for days, or all three.

Once the survey team has assembled the information and is familiar with it, the data must be organized. Specifically, the data must be sorted, cleaned, and entered into files. The files may be part of a qualitative data analysis

EXAMPLE 4.9
Sources of Qualitative Information and Sample Uses

Text (records of thoughts, feelings, values, and behaviors found in diaries, books, paintings, newspapers, sound recordings, videos, films): The surveyor reviews selected texts to look for common themes, answer questions about people's motivations, test hypotheses, or build theories.

Example: Two people are asked to review a sample of 10 years' worth of newsmagazines in order to examine how the advertisements in them depict women's changing roles over time.

- *Situation 1:* The reviewers are asked to characterize the women according to their roles. After completing the task, the reviewers meet to discuss their findings. Reviewer 1 has come up with 20 roles and Reviewer 2 has come up with 8. After discussion, the reviewers agree on 11 roles, including businesswoman, mother, and wife.

- *Situation 2:* The reviewers are given a list of categories, such as businesswoman, mother, and wife, and are asked to check off those that apply in each of the advertisements they examine.

Observations: One or more individuals watch people in action in natural settings (such as in their homes, schools, offices, communities). The observers may use structured forms to guide their observations; they may take notes on what they see, or they may film the events or otherwise record them.

Example: Two observers spend time in the waiting room of a large urban hospital's emergency department

Example 4.9 continued

in order to estimate how long patients there must wait to see a doctor.

Interviews: One or more people ask questions of others, face-to-face or on the telephone. Interviews may be conducted with individuals or groups. Sometimes, interviewers have only lists of topics to cover, whereas at other times, they have detailed guides containing all the topics and questions to be covered.

Example: An interviewer conducts a group interview with five people in transitional housing to find out about their experiences. Are the facilities adequate?

Example: Telephone interviews are conducted to find out people's views concerning the videotaping of executions.

Focus Groups: Focus group interviews explicitly include and use group interaction to generate data. The idea is to get people with similar needs or preferences to share them.

Example: A surveyor brings 10 people together to discuss ways of improving their mental health care at local community clinics. A trained moderator asks the questions, using a detailed guide.

Consensus Panels: A survey is conducted with a group of experts to get their opinions on social questions when little information exists or when the information available is contradictory. Consensus panels can be relatively informal or highly structured.

Example: A surveyor brings 14 experts in reading together to gain the benefit of their expertise on three approaches to teaching reading. The experts are given a list of scenarios and are asked to rate the appropriateness

Example 4.9 continued

of each reading method for the children described in each scenario. A skilled moderator leads the discussion. At the conclusion of the study, a report is issued describing where the experts agree and disagree.

computer software program or they may be composed of index cards (if the survey is very small). The computer files or index card files constitute the database.

The process of obtaining a clean database—that is, one that contains all the information in one place and in a usable form—is an integral part of the analysis process. Only clean data stand a chance of producing reliable and valid information.

You can clean qualitative data by checking to see that the coding of observations, narratives, and themes are consistent across survey team members and by setting rules for what to do about missing data. To avoid discrepancies in coding, you must train coders carefully and check the quality of their work on a regular basis. Computerized interview programs are designed to prevent miscoding in the field. However, computer-assisted interviews may not be appropriate in some qualitative survey settings (e.g., in a hospice or with young children).

Statistical techniques such as imputation and weighting can be applied to missing data in some qualitative surveys. *Imputing data* means estimating how respondents would have answered particular questions if they had chosen to. Suppose you are conducting a survey to find out about the effects of a tornado on the quality of life in a small community. Suppose also that one of the survey questions asks about the amount of money people in the community have spent on repairing tornado damage to their homes. Finally, suppose that after reviewing the surveys, you realize that about 12 of 50 interviewees did not answer the question on the amount they spent. Consider also that further review reveals that the question itself was missing from some of the surveys. Should you exclude the missing data? Or should you "guess" at what the responses might have been? One method of estimating what those 12 people who didn't respond would have reported is to identify other people in the sample with similar damage, compute the average costs, and assign those averages to the 12 people. The assumption is that the 12 nonrespondents are not likely to differ from the average in their spending.

Another approach to dealing with missing data or observations is to weight the responses. If you expect 50% of men and 50% of women to complete a survey, but only 40% of men do, you can weight men's returns so that they are equivalent to 50%. There are many strategies for weighting, among them logistic regression analysis. Weighting can be a complex activity, and you should not attempt it without appropriate statistical knowledge.

A content analysis may be *inductive* or *deductive*. In an inductive analysis, the surveyor goes through the database and looks for dominant themes. Using the processes of inductive reasoning and experience, the surveyor reviews the data for unifying ideas. As an example, consider an interviewer who has identified the themes shown in Example 4.10 after reviewing transcripts of discussions with minimum wage workers in restaurants, hotels, schools, and offices. The interviewer has gone through transcripts and has identified four themes, each of which has two subthemes. Subthemes are useful for providing more specific data than themes often do. In the case shown in Example 4.10, for instance, the interviewer can gain more precise information from analyzing workers' perceptions of their marital difficulties than from looking at their perceptions of their families (which may also include children and parents).

In a deductive analysis, the surveyor preselects themes and subthemes that he or she thinks are likely to occur. The surveyor then combs through the transcripts (or other data)

EXAMPLE 4.10
Themes Evoked by a Review
of Hypothetical Transcripts of Interviews
With Minimum Wage Workers

Themes	Subthemes
Financial	Paying for food, paying rent
	Providing for children's extra needs
Family	Marital difficulties
	Lack of day-care options
Health concerns	Health insurance
	Preventive care, such as eye exams
Self-concept	Respect from family
	Respect from society

and notes every instance of support for the preselected themes. The surveyor may count which themes or subthemes are repeated most frequently and place emphasis on those. The surveyor may also add to the list of themes and subthemes as additional ones emerge.

For small surveys, surveyors may be able to do content analysis "by hand," but for larger surveys, the use of computers is essential. Data management and analysis software programs assist surveyors in coding and in building conceptual models to describe the relationships among variables; they also produce numerical and other tables and graphs. There are many software options available, including a program provided free by the Centers for Disease Control (at www.cdc.gov; click on "software"). CDC EZ-Text is a software program designed to assist researchers in creating, managing, and analyzing semistructured qualitative databases. Most software developed for use in qualitative research is proprietary, so make sure your survey's budget includes the cost of the software and time for instruction in its use.

There are advantages to using both qualitative and statistical surveys, and both approaches have their own advocates. Neither survey type is inherently better than the other. Your choice between them should be dictated by your survey's purpose. If you are interested in designing a culturally appropriate intervention for newly arrived immigrants, for instance, a qualitative survey can provide you with cultural knowledge to use in planning the intervention. If you are part of a team concerned with evaluating the efficacy and safety of an intervention, you will rely on statistical methods.

Qualitative surveys, like statistical surveys, involve issues of design, sampling, and measurement validity. Questions such as the following are typical during the design stage of a qualitative survey: Who should be included in the interview (or focus group or consensus panel)? How many interviews should we conduct to get data? How can we be sure that the information we collect is valid? Should we have one observer or two? If we use two observers, what level of agreement between them is necessary before we can have confidence in their findings?

Qualitative surveys sometimes rely on **triangulation**, which is the collection of data from different sources (interviews and field notes) or from different surveyors in different places. The idea is that if multiple sources of information produce similar results, the credibility of the survey's findings are enhanced. Although triangulation sounds good, it can get to be very expensive to carry out, because each data collection method used adds to the costs of the survey.

For more information on statistical and qualitative data analysis and management, see **How to Manage, Analyze, and Interpret Survey Data** (Volume 9 in this series). The specific objectives of that volume are as follows:

- Organize and manage data for analysis
  - Draft an analysis plan
  - Define and format a data file
  - Create a codebook
  - Establish the reliability of the coding
  - Recognize techniques for dealing with incomplete or missing data and outliers and for recoding
- Identify methods for entering accurate data into spreadsheets, database management programs, and statistical programs
- Learn the use of analytic terms such as the following:
  - Distribution
  - Critical value
  - Skew
  - Transformation
  - Measures of central tendency
  - Dispersion
  - Variation
  - Statistical significance
  - Practical significance
  - p value

- Alpha

- Beta

- Linear

- Curvilinear

- Scatterplot

- Null hypothesis

- List the steps to follow in selecting an appropriate analytic method

- Distinguish among nominal, ordinal, and numerical scales and data so as to

  - Identify independent and dependent variables

  - Recognize the appropriate uses of the mean, median, and mode

  - Recognize the appropriate uses of the range, standard deviation, percentile rank, and interquartile range

  - Understand the logic in and uses of correlations and regression

  - Learn the steps in conducting and interpreting hypothesis tests

  - Compare and contrast hypothesis testing and the use of confidence intervals

  - Calculate the odds ratio and risk ratio

  - Understand the logic in and uses of the chi-square distribution and test

  - Understand the logic in and uses of the *t* test

- Understand the logic in and uses of analysis of variance

- Read and interpret computer output

■ Understand the basic steps in a content analysis of qualitative data

■ Conduct an analysis of open-ended questions asking people what they like least and best

5 Accurate Survey Reports

Fair and accurate reporting of survey results means staying within the boundaries set by the survey's design, sampling methods, data collection quality, and analysis. To present an accurate survey report, you need to know how to use lists, charts, and tables to display your data.

Lists

Lists are useful for stating survey objectives, methods, and findings. The lists shown in Example 5.1 come from a formal talk about a survey of job satisfaction conducted with part-time employees. Lists are simple to follow and so are very useful in survey reports.

Charts

A figure is a method of presenting data in graphic form, as in a diagram or chart. Pie, bar, and line charts are all different

EXAMPLE 5.1
Surveys and Lists

1. To State Survey Objectives

Survey of Part-Time Employees: Purpose is to find out

- Quality of life
- Characteristics of office environment
- Reasons for part-time employment

2. To Describe Survey Methods

Seven Tasks

- Conduct focus groups
- Identify specific objectives
- Set inclusion and exclusion criteria
- Adapt the PARTEE Survey
- Pilot-test and revise PARTEE
- Train interviewers
- Administer the interviews

3. To Report Survey Results or Findings

PARTEE's Results

62% STATE THAT PART-TIME EMPLOYMENT HAS IMPROVED THE QUALITY OF THEIR LIVES.

- No difference between men and women
- No difference between younger and older respondents

Example 5.1 continued

32% OF EMPLOYEES ARE
ALMOST ALWAYS SATISFIED.

- Men more satisfied

- No difference between younger and older
  respondents

kinds of figures. Each has its uses and rules of preparation, as illustrated below.

Pie charts such as the one in Figure 5.1 are useful for describing a survey's responses in percentages. As you can see, the *slices* in the pie chart show that the **response rates** in all four schools in the study in question were fairly equal, proportionately, in 2001, ranging from 23% to 27%. In 2002, Lincoln substantially increased its responses, so the range was much wider (from 11% to 41%), and the proportions were less similar among the schools.

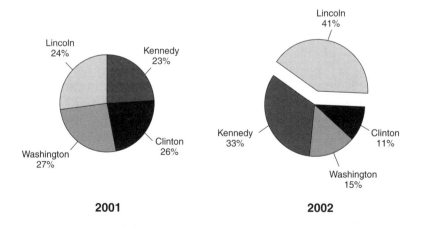

Figure 5.1. Attitudes Toward School

Figure 5.2 is an example of a bar chart. Any bar chart (or graph) depends on a horizontal X-axis and a vertical Y-axis. On the X-axis, you can put nearly any type of data (e.g., names, years, time of day, and age). The X-axis usually displays data on the independent variable. The Y-axis represents the unit of measurement, or dependent variable (e.g., dollars, scores, and number of people responding).

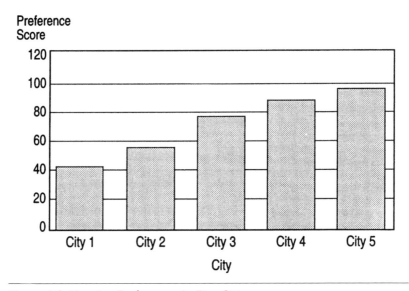

Figure 5.2. Housing Preferences in Five Cities
SOURCE: Housing Commission Mail Survey.

Bar charts are often used in survey reports because they are relatively easy to read and interpret. The bar chart in Figure 5.2 shows the results of a study of housing preferences in five cities. Notice that the figure has a title or caption ("Housing Preferences in Five Cities"), that both the X-axis and the Y-axis are labeled (cities and preference scores), and that the source of the data is given (the Housing Commission Mail Survey).

Figure 5.3 shows a line chart in which men's and women's job satisfaction is compared over a 10-year period. Because two groups (men and women) are involved in this job satisfaction survey, the figure includes a key (or legend) to the meanings of the different kinds of lines shown. The chart shows that men's satisfaction has been lower than women's for 9 of the 10 years. Only in 1998 were the positions reversed and men appeared more satisfied than women. We cannot be sure if this apparent difference is real, however. Only a statistical test (such as a *t* test comparing men's and women's average scores) can help determine the veracity of that assumption.

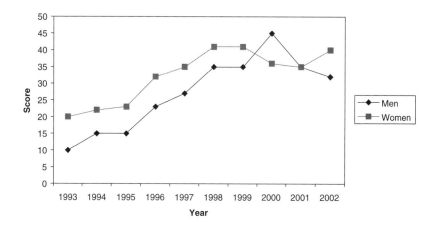

Figure 5.3. Job Satisfaction: A 10-Year Study
SOURCE: The Job Satisfaction Inventory.
NOTE: Higher scores are better.

Tables

Tables are also used frequently in survey reports, usually to summarize data about respondents and their responses and to compare survey results at one or more times. Suppose you are responsible for surveying workers in an experiment to find out if their health habits can be improved through an on-the-job health promotion program. One of Company A's two factories is randomly assigned to the experimental program. The other is assigned to the control condition, which consists of free lectures at the company's gym; attendance at the lectures is voluntary. Your main objectives in conducting the survey are to describe and compare the participants in the two programs and to compare their health habits (e.g., willingness to exercise regularly) before entering the program, immediately after, and 2 years later. If you achieve your objectives, you will produce tables that look like those in Example 5.2, with appropriate numbers and percentages filling out the empty "shells" in the example tables.

When should you use tables to report survey results? You will find them to be especially useful in written reports, because they provide detailed information for readers. Tables are also useful as visual aids when you are giving oral presentations. Unfortunately, little conclusive information is available to guide you in choosing to display survey results using charts versus tables. If you need to make a visual impact, then charts are appropriate. If you want to illustrate your points with numbers, then tables are appropriate. Often, it is best to use a mixture of tables and charts in a single report.

EXAMPLE 5.2
Shell Tables to Describe,
Compare, and Illustrate Changes

Description of participants in the experimental and control groups

The table will contain the number (*n*) and percentage of the sample (%) in the experimental group and in the control group of different ages (years), with varying exposures to education, who are male or female, and who speak primarily English, Russian, Spanish, or some other language at home.

	Experimental Group		Control Group	
	n	%	*n*	%
Age (years)				
Over 55				
45-55				
35-54				
34 or less				
Education				
Graduate school				
College				
High school				
Gender				
Male				
Female				
Primary language spoken at home				
English				
Russian				
Spanish				

Example 5.1 continued

Changes over time in the experimental and control groups: Willingness to exercise regularly

The shell table below is set up to show comparisons among scores on the 25-question Exercise Inventory for the number of people (n) in the experimental group and in the control group.

Timing	Average Scores on Exercise Inventory	
	Experimental Group	Control Group
	n	n
Before joining program		
Immediately after		
2 years after		

For more information about survey reports, see **How to Report on Surveys** (Volume 10 in this series). Objectives of that volume are as follows:

- Prepare, interpret, and explain lists, pie charts, and bar and line charts

- Prepare, interpret, and explain tables

- Identify survey report contents for

  - Oral presentations

  - Written presentations

  - Technical and academic audiences

  - General audiences

- Prepare computerized presentations

- Identify characteristics of good Internet survey reporting

- Explain what is on-screen in Internet survey reporting

- Explain in writing the contents and meaning of tables and figures

- Explain orally and in writing the survey's objectives, design, sample, psychometric properties, results, and conclusions

- Review reports for readability

- Review reports for comprehensiveness and accuracy

6 Ethical Surveys

Surveys are methods of collecting information about people's backgrounds, knowledge, attitudes, and behaviors. The people who participate in surveys are "human subjects" with whom you, the surveyor, interact. If you are conducting a survey for a private company or for commercial purposes, and the survey is supported only by company funds, you may not have to deal with strict rules to protect the rights of human subjects to their privacy. That does not mean you should ignore those rights, only that you probably do not have to adhere to strict written requirements. If you are conducting your survey for an institution or organization (even a private firm) that receives U.S. government support or as part of your work in an academic institution (even if you are a student), however, you are likely to have to prepare written documentation of your planned survey procedures for review by an institutional review board (IRB) before you can begin. IRBs are in charge of determining whether any kind of research, including survey research, is designed so as to guarantee that each participant's privacy and other rights are protected. If your institution's IRB finds that your survey meets its standards, you can proceed. If not, the IRB will not allow you to collect data.

Ethical Principles for the Protection of Human Subjects

In 1979, the National Commission for the Protection of Human Subjects of Biomedical and Behavioral Research published *The Belmont Report: Ethical Principles and Guidelines for the Protection of Human Subjects of Research*. This document is still regarded as the foundation of ethical research, including survey research. Three major principles come from **The Belmont Report:**

- *Respect for persons:* This principle incorporates at least two ethical convictions: first, that individuals should be treated as autonomous agents, and second, that persons with diminished autonomy are entitled to protection.

- *Beneficence:* This principle holds that researchers must treat subjects in an ethical manner, not only by respecting their decisions and protecting them from harm but also by actively making efforts to secure their well-being.

- *Justice:* This principle concerns the balance for subjects between receiving the benefits of research and bearing its burdens. For example, to ensure justice, researchers need to examine their selection of research subjects in order to determine whether they are systematically choosing persons from some classes (e.g., welfare recipients, persons in institutions) simply because of those persons' easy availability rather than for reasons directly related to the problems being studied.

Institutional Review Boards

Institutional review boards are administrative bodies that are charged with protecting the rights and welfare of human research subjects. Most IRBs are concerned with research activities conducted under the auspices of institutions such as schools and universities, but many private companies and foundations have IRBs also.

According to the U.S. government, all IRB activities related to human subject research should be guided by the ethical principles laid out in *The Belmont Report.* U.S. government policy also mandates that an IRB have at least five members and that members should have varying backgrounds. When selecting IRB members, institutions must take into account the racial and cultural makeup of the board and must be sensitive to community attitudes. In addition to possessing the professional competence necessary to review specific research activities, IRB members must also be able to ascertain the acceptability of proposed research in terms of institutional commitments and regulations, applicable law, and standards of professional conduct and practice. U.S. government policy also requires that if an IRB regularly reviews research that involves a vulnerable category of subjects (such as children, prisoners, pregnant women, or handicapped or mentally disabled persons), the institution for which it functions must consider including on the IRB one or more individuals who are knowledgeable about and experienced in working with these subjects. Also, an institution must make every effort to ensure that its IRB does not consist entirely of men or entirely of women.

It is not unusual for IRBs to consider all of the criteria in the following list in determining whether or not particular surveys can be implemented.

Informed Consent

PURPOSE

Survey participants must give their **informed consent** before taking part in a survey; that is, they can formally agree to participate only after they have been informed

Criteria Typically Used
by Institutional Review Boards

- **Study design:** Many experts agree that IRBs should approve only research that is both valid and of value. A poorly designed study will necessarily lead to misleading results. Study design includes subject recruitment, selection, and assignment to groups; survey reliability and validity; and data analysis.

- **Risks and benefits:** IRBs evaluate whether the risks to subjects are reasonable in relation to the anticipated benefits, if any, to the subjects, as well as the importance of the knowledge reasonably expected to result from the research.

- **Equitable selection of subjects:** IRBs usually consider the purpose of the research and the setting of the survey and closely examine any planned research involving vulnerable subject populations, such as children, prisoners, persons with cognitive disorders, and persons who are economically or educationally disadvantaged.

- **Identification of subjects and confidentiality:** IRBs are required to review researchers' planned methods for identification of subjects. This includes examination of the means of identifying and contacting potential subjects and the methods to be used in ensuring subjects' privacy and confidentiality.

- **Qualifications:** IRBs examine the qualifications of surveyors and their survey teams. In addition, IRBs consider the adequacy of the facilities and equipment to be used to conduct the research and maintain the rights and welfare of the subjects.

- ■ **Informed consent:** The informed consent process is often the heart of the matter. IRBs usually focus a great deal of their attention on researchers' plans to gain the informed consent of their subjects.

about the risks and benefits of participation, the activities that constitute participation, the terms of their participation, and their rights as research subjects.

The *informed consent form* provides potential research subjects with sufficient written information to guide them in deciding whether or not to participate in a research study. After presenting this information, the researcher usually obtains consent in writing by having the subject sign the form. If for some reason a person agrees to participate but does not sign a consent form, the researcher needs to document the fact that the material in the form was administered (say, on the phone) and that the participant understood it. The consent form is designed to protect all parties: the subject, the investigator, and the institution. Therefore, it is important that it present information in an organized and easily understood format.

CONTENTS OF AN INFORMED CONSENT FORM

The specific items on informed consent forms vary from institution to institution, but the principles behind them do not. Example 6.1 shows the various elements contained in a typical informed consent form.

Notice that the participant is given a copy of the consent form. In mail (whether sent via e-mail or post) survey studies, completed and returned questionnaires themselves may (depending on the IRB and the purpose of the survey) be considered evidence of informed consent. Mail survey participants sometimes neglect to send the informed consent forms back with their questionnaires.

Researcher Misconduct

Researcher misconduct is becoming an increasingly important concern throughout the world. Documenting such misconduct (if it occurs) is currently an issue for all surveyors who work in academic institutions and in organizations that receive funding from the U.S. government. Example 6.2 lists some problematic behaviors on the part of researchers that may occur in many situations in which surveys are conducted.

Faking the data is a clear example of researcher misconduct. More subtle examples include cases such as the following:

- A researcher exaggerates a survey's findings to support his or her own point of view.

- A researcher changes survey protocol without informing the IRB beforehand.

- A researcher fails to maintain adequate documentation of the survey's methodology (such as preparing a codebook).

- A researcher releases participant information without permission to do so.

- A researcher undertakes a study although he or she knows there are insufficient resources to complete the study as promised.

- A researcher has financial or other interests in common with the funders or supporters of the research (conflict of interest).

EXAMPLE 6.2
Some Problematic Researcher Behaviors

Problematic Behavior	Definition
• Misconduct	• Fabrication or falsification of data; plagiarism
• Questionable research practices	• Actions that violate values of research and may be detrimental to the research process but do not directly threaten the integrity of the research record (examples include failing to retain research records for a reasonable period or using inappropriate statistics to enhance findings)
• Other misconduct not pertaining to scientific integrity	• Unacceptable behaviors that are subject to generally applicable legal and social penalties, but are not unique to research (examples include sexual harassment, misuse of funds, violations of federal regulations)
• Other misconduct pertaining to scientific integrity	• Unacceptable behavior that does not directly affect the integrity of the research process, but is nevertheless directly associated with misconduct in science (examples include covering up scientific misconduct and carrying out reprisals against whistle-blowers)
• Sloppiness	• Negligent or irregular research practices that risk distortion of the research record, although such distortion is not the researcher's intention

7 Reasonable Resources

A survey's resources are reasonable if they adequately cover the financial costs and time needed for all activities of the survey to be conducted in the time planned. The elements you need to consider include the costs of, and time for, hiring and training staff, preparing and validating the survey form, gaining IRB approval, administering the survey, and analyzing, interpreting, and reporting the findings.

How much does it cost to conduct a survey? How can you be sure that you have an adequate amount of resources (time and money) to conduct your survey? Novice surveyors and experts alike often ask these questions. You can answer them by first answering seven other questions:

1. What are the survey's major tasks?

2. What skills are needed to complete each task?

3. How much time is available to complete the survey?

4. How much time does each task take?

5. Who can be hired to perform each task?

6. What are the costs of each task?

7. What additional resources are needed?

The meanings of these questions and how you can go about answering them are discussed and illustrated in the sections that follow.

What Needs to Be Done?

A survey is a system for collecting information. Conducting a survey study involves deciding on the objectives of the survey, developing a survey instrument, designing a study and identifying the sample, administering the survey, and analyzing and reporting the results. You might use the following checklist of typical survey tasks as a guide as you go about determining the tasks you must complete in conducting your own survey. Each of the tasks on the checklist is explained below.

Checklist of Typical Survey Tasks

✓ Identify the survey's objectives.

- Conduct focus groups to identify the objectives.

- Obtain official approval of the objectives.

- Conduct a review of the literature to define terms and justify theory underlying the survey questions.

✓ Design the survey.

- Choose a survey design (e.g., descriptive or experimental).

- Decide on a sample.

✓ Prepare the survey instrument.

- Identify existing and appropriate instruments.

- Conduct a literature review.

- Contact other surveyors.

- Adapt some or all questions from existing instruments.

- Prepare a new instrument.

✓ Prepare documents for the IRB.

- Develop an informed consent form.

- Justify the survey and describe its purposes, methods, and procedures for privacy and confidentiality.

✓ Pilot-test the instrument.

- Conduct a cognitive pretest.

- Identify the sample for the pilot test.

- Obtain permission for the pilot test.

- Analyze the pilot-test data.

Checklist of Typical Survey Tasks Continued

- ■ Revise the instrument to make it final.

✓ Administer the survey.

- ■ Hire staff.

- ■ Train staff.

- ■ Monitor the quality of administration.

- ■ Retrain staff.

- ■ Send out mail, supervise the questionnaire, and conduct interviews.

- ■ Follow up.

✓ Manage the data.

- ■ Code responses.

- ■ Prepare a codebook.

- ■ Consult with a programmer.

- ■ Train data enterers.

- ■ Enter the data.

- ■ Run a preliminary analysis.

- ■ Clean the data.

- ■ Prepare a final codebook.

✓ Analyze the data.

- Prepare an analysis plan.

- Analyze the psychometric properties of the instrument.

- Analyze the results of the survey.

✓ Report the results.

- Write the report.

- Have the report reviewed.

- Modify the report based on the reviews.

- Prepare the presentation.

- Present the report orally.

Getting Each Survey Task Done

IDENTIFYING SURVEY OBJECTIVES

A survey's objectives are its particular purposes or hoped-for outcomes. In general, surveys gather data that can be used to describe, compare, or explain knowledge, attitudes, and behavior. For example, a survey can be designed to get information that will describe customer satisfaction in Stores A and B, compare satisfaction in A and B, and explain why satisfaction is higher in A than in B.

What are the particular objectives of a survey? For example, in a customer satisfaction survey, should the aim be to compare younger and older persons in their satisfaction? Should information be collected about education or region of the country so that satisfaction can be compared among people with differing levels of education who live in various parts of the country? Methods for answering questions like these include conducting focus groups and reviewing the literature.

Once you have identified your survey's objectives, you should certify them "officially." For example, suppose you intend to survey customers and compare satisfaction among men and women of differing educational attainment. Will the information you gain meet the needs of the users of the survey? One way to find out is to create an advisory group of potential users of the survey. This group may consist of three to five people who can assist you in keeping the survey on target.

Example 7.1 illustrates how objectives were set for one particular survey of responses to natural disasters.

EXAMPLE 7.1
Setting Survey Objectives:
What Needs to Be Done?

The Center for Natural Disaster Control and Prevention plans to survey victims of floods, fires, earthquakes, and tornadoes. Responses to a mailed questionnaire will be supplemented with interviews. Data from the survey are to be used to determine how public agencies can most effectively respond to victims immediately after a natural disaster. What should the survey want to find out? In other words, what should its objectives be?

The survey team first conducts a review of the literature to see how other researchers have defined the term *victim* and to determine if other surveys of disaster victims are available, and, if so, what their objectives are. The team then convenes a six-member focus group that consists of three people who have lived through one or

Example 7.1 continued

more natural disasters, a psychiatrist whose expertise is in treating people with posttraumatic stress disorder, and two members of the Agency for Emergency Relief.

Based on the review of the literature and the focus group results, the survey team decides to use a mail survey and sets the following four survey objectives:

1. Describe psychological damage associated with the disaster

2. Describe physical damage to person, home, business, school, and so on

3. Identify needs for services during the disaster (for victims of fires and floods)

4. Identify needs for services immediately and 6 months after the disaster

The list of objectives is sent for approval to the advisory board, which recommends that Objective 4 be amended to read as follows:

4. Identify needs for services within 3 months of the disaster and 12 to 18 months after

DESIGNING THE SURVEY

The objectives of the survey guide the design. For example, if one of your survey objectives is to identify needs for services within 3 months of a natural disaster and 12 to 18 months after, then you know that you must conduct a longitudinal survey. This means you will be collecting data over time (in this case, twice: within 3 months of the disaster and then between 12 and 18 months after the disaster). If the objective is to make comparisons, then the survey's design will include two or more groups of respondents.

The next issue you must resolve is whether you plan to survey everyone or just a sample. If you sample, you must decide on a sampling strategy (see Example 7.2).

EXAMPLE 7.2
Survey Design:
What Needs to Be Done?

The Center for Natural Disaster Control and Prevention's survey team decides to conduct a mail survey of a cohort of victims in three states: California, Missouri, and Tennessee. (A cohort is a group of respondents who share an experience or other characteristic, such as loss of a home to an earthquake, that is central to the objectives of a survey.)

Four cohorts will be surveyed. In California, there will be two: fire victims and earthquake victims; in Missouri, flood victims; and in Tennessee, tornado victims. To find out how many people should be in each cohort, the survey team's statistician conducts a special analysis and finds that at least 50 people are needed in each cohort. Because the study is a longitudinal survey, the statistician recommends beginning with 75 in each cohort, on the assumption that as many as 25 people may drop out, move, or become inaccessible because of illness or other reasons.

PREPARING THE SURVEY INSTRUMENT

Once you have set your objectives, you need to create the survey instrument. You should first consult both the literature and other surveyors to find out if any instruments are available that will serve to help you meet your objectives.

If you are lucky, you may find a survey instrument that is designed to collect data that meet the needs of your survey's objectives and that also can be obtained, administered, and scored in a timely and efficient way. You still must check to see that the instrument is appropriate for your population. Is the reading level appropriate? Does the survey ask for all the information you need? Has it been tried out with a population similar to your own? Can you obtain the survey instrument in time? Will you have to pay for it, and, if so, can you afford the price? If you decide to adopt an instrument that is already in use, you need to check the directions to the user and administrator to make sure that they are satisfactory for your purposes.

The most important consideration in adapting a survey instrument is whether it is the type you need. If you want to conduct telephone interviews but the instrument is in the form of a self-administered questionnaire, you must be sure you have the resources to translate it from one type of survey to the other.

If you decide to prepare some or all of your own instrument, you will have to outline the content, select response formats (e.g., ratings on a scale from *very positive* to *very negative*), and prepare rules for administration and scoring.

Example 7.3 shows how one survey team prepares a self-administered questionnaire to find out about people's reactions to natural disasters.

GETTING READY FOR THE IRB

Institutional review boards are charged with deciding whether individual surveys are designed in such a way that they protect the rights of participants or subjects. Most large institutions involved in conducting research, such as universities, hospitals, and other private and public organizations, have IRBs that review all proposed research studies, including survey studies. Any organization that receives funding from the U.S. government is required to have an IRB's

EXAMPLE 7.3
Preparing a Self-Administered Questionnaire: What Needs to Be Done?

The Center for Natural Disaster Control and Prevention's survey team reviews the literature on natural disasters, focusing on reports published by government emergency agencies to identify survey instruments. Team members identify 20 appropriate survey instruments and are able to obtain 15 of these within the 1-month period allocated for the literature review. The team decides that none of the surveys is wholly appropriate, but 10 of the surveys contain at least one question that may be adapted or used in its entirety.

The team members prepare an outline of their survey's content and decide to ask questions that have the following format:

Where were you when the earthquake struck?	Please circle ONE response.	
My own home	Yes	No
Someone else's home	Yes	No
Traveling on a city street	Yes	No
Traveling on the freeway	Yes	No
In an office building	Yes	No
In a restaurant	Yes	No
Other (specify) _____	Yes	No

approval before allowing data to be collected, whether the data collector is a student or an experienced investigator.

An essential part of the protection of human subjects is the concept of informed consent. Usually, when you go through the IRB process in preparing to conduct a survey study, you must present to the IRB written documents describing the rationale for the survey and its objectives as well as your planned sample selection, research design, and data collection procedures. In addition, you must provide the IRB with a copy of the informed consent form you will be having participants sign. If you plan to obtain informed consent over the telephone for telephone interviews, then you will have to present the written script to the IRB. If you plan to conduct observations, you will need to give the IRB a written statement affirming that you will not use any photographs or other audio and visual materials you gather in any way without participants' permission.

Preparing the documents you need for the IRB may take weeks, and getting them accepted may take months. While you are waiting for approval, you are ethically (and legally) bound not to collect any data. Further, if, during the course of the survey, you decide to change the study's protocol—for example, you want to add telephone interviews to an e-mail survey—you must inform the IRB of the change and gain approval before proceeding. (For more about IRBs and informed consent, see Chapter 6.)

COGNITIVE PRETESTING OF THE INSTRUMENT

A cognitive pretest is a chance to take a draft of your survey to potential respondents and ask them individually to review each question: What does the question mean to the respondent? Is there a better way of asking it? What do the response choices mean? Given a choice between two types of response formats, which is better? When the people you are planning to survey are not native English speakers, you can ask, What is a better way of getting these ideas across in your language?

You should choose the respondents for your cognitive pretest based on their similarity to your future respondents in background and skills. If you plan on surveying men and women, you should include both in the pretest. How many people you can include will depend on how much time and money you have. Remember that you need to have time and resources remaining after the pretest to redo some of the survey questions based on your pretest findings. You may even need to conduct several pretests before you come up with the final survey.

PILOT-TESTING THE INSTRUMENT

A **pilot test** is an opportunity to try out an instrument well before it is made final. Unlike in a pretest, in a pilot test you try to simulate the use of the survey instrument in its intended setting. As in a pretest, in a pilot test you should monitor the ease with which respondents complete the questionnaire and also the ease with which you can administer and score the instrument.

Usually, for a pilot test you need 10 or more people who are willing to complete the survey. You should ask each of them if he or she understands the directions for completing the survey and each of the questions, as well as whether the wording of the questions and the places to mark responses are clear.

You should also use the pilot test to examine the logistics of administering the survey instrument. This is particularly important with interviews. Can interviewers follow the directions that are on the survey form? How long does it take for them to record responses? Do they know what to do with completed interviews? For example, how many interviews should they complete before they return the questionnaires to the survey team's office? How many phone calls should an interviewer make to one potential respondent before giving up? You can use the questions in the following list to guide your pilot testing.

For pilot testing to be effective, you should use respondents who are similar to those who will be asked to participate in the survey. If your survey is targeted to parents of

(text continues on page 112)

Questions to Ask When
Pilot-Testing Survey Instruments

Mail and other self-administered questionnaires (including those administered via e-mail and the Internet)

- Are instructions for completing the survey clearly written?

- Are questions easy to understand?

- Do respondents know how to indicate responses (e.g., circle or mark the response; use a special pencil; use the space bar)?

- Are the response choices mutually exclusive?

- Are the response choices exhaustive?

- In a mail survey, do respondents understand what to do with completed questionnaires (e.g., return them by mail in a self-addressed envelope; fax them)?

- In a mail survey, do respondents understand when to return the completed questionnaires?

- In a computer-assisted survey, can respondents correctly use the commands?

- In a computer-assisted survey, do respondents know how to change (or "correct") their answers?

- If you are giving an incentive for completing the survey, do respondents understand how to obtain it

(continued)

(e.g., it will automatically be sent upon receipt of completed survey; it is included with the questionnaire)?

- Is the privacy of the respondents respected and protected?

- Do respondents have any suggestions regarding the addition or deletion of questions, clarification of instructions, or improvements in questionnaire format?

Telephone interviews

- Do interviewers understand how to ask questions and present options for responses?

- Do interviewers know how to get in-depth information, when appropriate, by probing respondents' brief answers?

- Do interviewers know how to record information?

- Do interviewers know how to code information?

- Do interviewers know how to keep interviews to the agreed-on time limit?

- Do interviewers know how to return completed interviews?

- Are interviewers able to select the sample using the agreed-on instructions?

- Can interviewers readily use the phone logs to record the number of times and when potential respondents were contacted?

- Do interviewees understand the questions?

- Do interviewees understand how to answer the questions (e.g., pick the top two; rate items according to whether they agree or disagree)?

- Do interviewees agree that their privacy has been protected and respected?

In-person interviews

- Do interviewers understand how to ask questions and present options for responses?

- Do interviewers know how to get in-depth information, when appropriate, by probing respondents' brief answers?

- Do interviewers know how to record information?

- Do interviewers know how to keep interviews to the agreed-on time limit?

- Do interviewers know how to return completed interviews?

- Do interviewees understand the questions?

- Do interviewees understand how to answer the questions (e.g., pick the top two; rate items according to whether they agree or disagree)?

- Do interviewees agree that their privacy has been protected and respected?

teenage children, for example, then your pilot-test sample should be made up of parents of teenage children.

The results of your pilot test should guide you in revising your survey instrument and planning the logistics of survey administration. Sometimes, surveyors must conduct more than one pilot test; this is costly.

A field test is a minitrial of the actual survey. For example, a field test of a survey of teenagers' use of health services is conducted in one state, and the results are then used to guide any revisions of the instrument and procedures before the final version of the survey is used in a nationwide study.

ADMINISTERING THE SURVEY

Administering a survey includes mailing the survey instrument and supervising its use (say, in a classroom) or conducting interviews. To administer a telephone survey properly, the interviewer must ask questions, record answers, keep records, stay within a time limit, and respect the respondent. To administer a mail survey, the surveyor must package the questionnaires (e.g., including self-addressed, stamped envelopes for respondents to return the questionnaires in and ensuring that respondents have enough time to complete all questions), follow up with people who do not respond by the due date, and, in some situations, handle the distribution of rewards and incentives for completed surveys. To administer a survey via e-mail or the World Wide Web, the surveyor must establish passwords, get programming help, and consult with experts concerning online security.

A poorly administered survey invariably leads to garbled responses and poor response rates. To ensure high-quality administration, you must be sure that all staff members are well trained and monitored. Before you hire staff members, you need to decide on the skills they must have in advance of training. For example, do you want people who can speak a certain language? Who can work certain hours? Be sure to take sufficient time to train staff thoroughly. You should conduct formal training sessions, give each trainee a written manual, and provide time for interviewers to practice conducting interviews. When survey administration begins, you should monitor staff performance (e.g., by observing a sample of interviews). If an interviewer's work is unsatisfactory, you should immediately retrain him or her.

MANAGING THE DATA

Data management begins with the first returned surveys. Are all the questions on the survey answered? If some data are missing, are some survey questions consistently at fault? Items may be troublesome if they are poorly worded or difficult to read.

One major data management activity is preparing the codebook, a document that contains the definitions of all the variables (age, for example), the values for those variables (e.g., for age, 10 years of age and younger; 11 years and older), and the locations of the variables and their values (often expressed as numbers in columns, in spreadsheet style). The codebook is a key component of a survey's documentation.

Data entry is also a major part of data management. You can enter survey data into a computer spreadsheet or statistical program. All statistical programs can verify the accuracy of entry, but it is always wise to use skilled data enterers. In computer-assisted, online, or scanned surveys with closed questions, data entry is automatic. That is, all answers are routinely stored in a database. If you use open-ended questions to gather qualitative data, you must make sure that your coders are well trained, because the codes they enter are the data. If you doubt that your coders are trained well enough for this task, ask them simply to record verbatim answers to questions; you can do the coding and interpretation later.

Managing data also includes checking for missing responses and missing surveys. You may need to use statistical techniques to compensate for gaps in the data if you have very many incomplete or missing surveys.

ANALYZING THE DATA

You can begin to plan for data analysis after you are sure of your survey objectives and you know whether the data will be nominal, ordinal, or numerical, and whether you can explain and justify the quality of the data. Suppose Surveyor 1 wants to compare boys and girls in their willingness to choose future careers in politics. Suppose also that in the data analysis, the number of positive answers to a self-administered questionnaire determines willingness and a score of 100 is considered twice as good as a score of 50. If the survey data are of high quality (e.g., all respondents answer all survey questions on a valid measure) and the data are numerical and continuous, then a t test might be the appropriate analytic method for making the comparison. Suppose, however, that Surveyor 2 takes a different approach to analyzing the extent of willingness to choose a career in politics. Surveyor 2 decides that positive willingness is a score of 50 or greater and negative willingness is a score of 49 or less. Assuming the data can be dichotomized (divided into two parts), Surveyor 2 might use a chi-square analysis to compare the number of boys and girls with scores of 49 and below with the number of those with scores of 50 and above.

Aside from providing survey results (e.g., data on how boys and girls compare in their willingness to choose careers in politics), data analysis can be used to determine the survey instrument's psychometric properties. How do you demonstrate that a score of 100 is twice as good as a score of 50, as posited by Surveyor 1? Stating with certainty that a survey has a scale with equal intervals (e.g., a score of 5 is half the value of a score of 10) requires the kind of analytic proof that psychometricians can provide. Psychometricians are skilled in statistically interpreting the reliability and validity of surveys.

REPORTING THE RESULTS

Once they have analyzed their data, surveyors typically write and disseminate reports or present them orally. First drafts are rarely acceptable; most reports of survey results go through many reviews and revisions before they are widely disseminated. When presenting oral reports, surveyors often find that visual aids such as slides or computer-aided graphic presentations can facilitate audiences' understanding of survey findings. Word processing and spreadsheet programs include table-making and graphic functions that are often helpful for presenting results. Also, most office software packages (which give users access to designs available on the Internet) offer sufficient graphics for the average presentation. More sophisticated programs are available too, of course.

Who Will Do It, and What Resources Are Needed? Personnel, Time, and Money

A survey happens because one or more persons take responsibility for completing the required tasks. In a very small survey study, one or two persons may be in charge of designing the survey, developing the survey instrument, administering it, analyzing the data, and reporting the results. In larger studies, teams of individuals with differing skills are involved. Sometimes, surveys are planned and conducted by survey team members with the assistance of consultants who are called in for advice or to complete very specific activities.

To begin your survey project, you need first to plan the activities and tasks that will have to be completed. Once you have accomplished this, you must decide on the skills required for each task. Next, you must decide what specific personnel or job descriptions are likely to find you people who have as many of the skills you need as efficiently as possible. For example, suppose your survey design requires that the survey team include someone with experience in training interviewers and writing survey questions. You may just happen to know someone who needs a job and has both these skills, but if you do not know the right person, knowing the skills required for the tasks in question will help you target your search.

The specific resources needed for any given surveys vary according to the survey's size and scope and the number of skills and personnel needed to accomplish each task. Example 7.4 lists the types of skills and resources needed for a "typical" survey. The individual elements shown in the example are discussed below.

SURVEY TASKS, SKILLS, AND RESOURCES

Identify Survey Objectives

Your first task is to identify your survey's objectives. If you use focus groups to help you identify objectives, you will need special expertise in conducting them and interpreting the results. Sometimes, focus group participants are remunerated financially; almost always, they receive refreshments. Other costs that you might incur in conducting focus groups include those associated with renting a meeting room, transporting participants, and preparing materials, such as literature reviews and survey questionnaires.

You may decide to use an advisory group to help you to obtain approval of the design and objectives of your survey. This may add costs in several ways; you may need resources for honoraria, mail and telephone contacts with advisors, and transportation of advisors to and from meetings.

If you decide to conduct a literature review as an aid to identifying your survey's objectives, you will need someone with expertise in identifying relevant sources of information from a variety of places (e.g., electronic databases, libraries, and public and private agencies), abstracting the information,

(text continues on page 120)

EXAMPLE 7.4
Typical Survey Tasks, Skills, and Resources

Survey Task	Skills Needed	Resources
1. Identify survey objectives	Conduct focus groups	Honoraria for participants Transportation for participants Room rental for meeting Refreshments Materials to guide discussion
	Convene advisors	Honoraria Telephone Mail
	Conduct literature review	Librarian Reproduction of materials Standardization of forms for recording contents of literature Training reviewers
2. Design the survey	Know alternative research designs and their implementation Have technical expertise in selecting sampling methods, determining sample size, and selecting samples	Appropriate analytic software

Example 7.4 continued

Survey Task	Skills Needed	Resources
3. Prepare the survey instrument	Conduct literature reviews Knowledge of target population Knowledge of questionnaire construction and organization	Reference manager for literature review Software for question and questionnaire design
4. Prepare materials for the IRB	Knowledge of ethical and legal issues Understanding of survey design and implementation Competent writer	
5. Conduct a cognitive pretest	Ability to communicate with participants Skill in recording and interpreting notes	Space to conduct pretest Refreshments Honoraria
6. Pilot-test the instrument	Ability to analyze pilot-test data Ability to interpret data	Analytic software and/or data entry program Data analyst

Example 7.4 continued

Survey Task	Skills Needed	Resources
	Interviews	
7. Administer the survey	Ask questions in a standardized, efficient manner	Materials for training Computers Telephone Quality-of-care system
	If using a computer-assisted survey, ability to code answers in a standardized manner	
	Self-administered	
	Understand logistics of mail surveys (e.g., include self-addressed, stamped envelope)	Postage, envelopes, reproduction
	Understand technical abilities and resources of participants	Programmer Computers for use by participants Web design (including provisions to ensure privacy)
8. Manage the data	Code data Enter data Clean data Create a codebook	Programmer Statistician: how to handle missing data and nonresponse

Example 7.4 continued

Survey Task	Skills Needed	Resources
9. Analyze the data	Select appropriate data analysis methods Perform data analysis Select appropriate psychometric methods Conduct appropriate psychometric analysis	Programmer Statistician Software
10. Report the results	Write report Prepare presentation Present report	Reproduction Postage for disseminating report (mail and express) Travel to present report Honoraria for reviewers, editors Graphics consultant

and displaying the results in a usable form. If more than one person is involved in abstracting information, you should provide a standardized form, so that all abstractors are seeking the same types of information. Special expertise is needed to prepare an abstraction form. Additionally, abstractors should be trained to use the form by an experienced educator, and the quality of their work should be monitored. Training may need to take place more than once; depending on the survey, training may be accomplished in 1 hour or may require 2 days. For example, 2-day training sessions are not unusual for large surveys of the literature regarding effective social programs and medical treatments. If your literature review is extensive, you should use a reference manager software system to store the bibliography.

Design the Survey

Expertise in research methodology is essential in designing a survey. At the design stage, decisions must be made concerning the appropriate intervals in a longitudinal study, the inclusion and exclusion criteria for survey participants, and the makeup of appropriate and meaningful comparison groups.

Sampling is usually considered one of the most technical of all survey tasks, because one must have knowledge of statistics to be able to decide on a sample size, choose and implement a sampling technique, and determine the adequacy of the sample and the generalizability of the results. Large survey teams include experts in research design and sampling; smaller surveys sometimes rely on expert consultants.

Whenever technical activities are to take place, you would be wise to check on the adequacy of the computer hardware and software available to your survey team. If they are not appropriate, you may need to pursue upgrades of computers or programs. In some cases, you may find that the existing computer facilities are adequate, but you may need special expertise in some areas, such as programming, to meet the particular needs of your survey.

Prepare the Survey Instrument

If the survey instrument is to be adapted from an already existing instrument, you will need expertise in conducting literature reviews to find out if any potentially useful instruments are available. Sometimes, a reasonably good survey is available: Why spend time and money to prepare an instrument if a valid one exists? It helps if you have experience in the subject matter you are addressing in your survey and know who is working in the field and might either have instruments or questions or know where and how to get them.

Selecting items from existing surveys or rewording them to fit into a new survey requires special skills. You need someone who has both knowledge regarding your respondents' reading levels and motivations to complete the survey and experience in writing survey questions and placing them in a questionnaire.

Preparing an entirely new instrument is daunting. Any job description in an advertisement for an instrument writer would call for excellent writing skills and knowledge of the topic of the survey.

Prepare Materials for the IRB

The institutional review board will typically require a written explanation of your study plans (including rationale, purposes, and methods), copies of one or more informed consent forms, and a copy of the survey instrument. Preparing the packet for the IRB is similar to writing a proposal. To accomplish this task, you need someone who can write well and who understands the methods you plan to use in your study. Many IRBs require detailed written explanations of why each survey question was chosen, how a study's participants are to be selected, and how the researcher plans to ensure the privacy of all respondents.

Conduct a Cognitive Pretest

To conduct a cognitive pretest of the survey instrument, you need to identify a sample of people who are willing to go through each question with you and tell you what it means to them. Do these participants understand the questions in the same way you do? Usually, surveyors conduct pretests with early versions of their surveys, and so some glitches are expected. Pretests almost always take the form of interviews, and they should be conducted in a quiet setting by a trained interviewer who follows strict rules for recording participants' answers. You will need experienced personnel to interpret pretest results and translate them into survey improvements.

Pilot-Test the Instrument

Pilot testing of the survey instrument is carried out with a group of potential respondents who are willing to try to complete a questionnaire that may be difficult to understand. You will need someone who has expertise in analyzing data to conduct an analysis of the data from the pilot test; it is also essential that this person have experience in interpreting survey participants' responses. Additionally, you will need someone who knows how to incorporate the findings of the pilot test into a more final version of the survey instrument.

Pilot testing may be very simple—say, a 1-hour tryout by a teacher in the classroom—or very complicated, involving many people, training, room rental, and so on. Also, the survey instrument, even for a pilot test, must be prepared in a readable, user-friendly format. You may need to get some assistance with creating the instrument's physical design.

Administer the Survey

To administer face-to-face, telephone, or computer-assisted interviews, you will need skilled and trained personnel. Interviewers must be able to elicit the information called for on the survey instrument as well as record or code the answers in appropriate ways. Interviewers must be able to talk to respondents and potential respondents in a courteous manner and to listen carefully. Also, they must talk and listen efficiently. If an interview is intended to last no longer than 10 minutes, the interviewer must adhere to that time frame. Interviews become increasingly costly and even unreliable when they exceed their planned duration.

Among the types of skills an individual requires to put together a mail questionnaire are the ability to prepare a mailing that is user-friendly (e.g., includes a self-addressed envelope) and the ability to monitor returns and conduct follow-ups with those not responding. Similar skills are required to conduct an e-mail survey: The survey must be user-friendly, responses need to be tracked, and nonrespondents need to be followed up.

If you plan to conduct Internet-based surveys, you should consider becoming familiar with commercial software packages that guide online survey preparation and analysis. If your project does not have a survey research specialist, you may need some training in the use of such software. If your survey is to be done at a local site (business, school, clinic), then privacy concerns associated with using the Internet may be especially daunting.

To administer any survey successfully, you will need expertise in defining the skills and abilities needed to administer the survey and in selecting people who are likely to master the needed skills. Training of survey team personnel is the key to getting reliable and valid survey data. For example, a poorly trained telephone interviewer is likely to get fewer responses than a well-trained interviewer. Because of the importance of training, many researchers who conduct large surveys use educational experts to assist them in designing instructional materials and programs.

In large and long-term surveys, researchers must monitor the quality of the interviews regularly. Are interviewers continuing to follow instructions? Are some forgetting to return completed interviews at the conclusion of each 2-day session? If deficiencies in the survey process are noted, retraining may be necessary.

To conduct telephone interviews, of course surveyors must have telephones. Established survey centers have phone banks as well as systems for computer-assisted, random-digit dialing. To conduct face-to-face interviews, surveyors need space for privacy and quiet. Mail surveys can consume large quantities of postage and paper. All types of surveys may include monetary and other incentives to encourage respondents to answer questions.

Administering computer-assisted interviews requires extensive programming and interviewer training. Interviewers need to be taught to code open-ended questions. They may also need to learn what to do when they encounter technical glitches, such as when the computer freezes during an interview.

Manage the Data

Managing the data includes programming, coding, and data entry, as well as setting up a database. Programming requires relatively high-level computer skills. Coding can be very complicated, too, especially if response categories are not precoded. Training and computer skills are needed to ensure that data enterers are expert in their tasks. Finally, data cleaning can be a highly skilled task involving important decisions, regarding what to do about missing data, for example.

Analyze the Data

Appropriate and justifiable data analysis is dependent on statistical and computer skills. Some surveys are very small and require only the computation of frequencies (number and percentages) or averages. Most, however, require comparisons among groups or predictions and explanations of findings. Furthermore, surveys of attitudes, values, beliefs, and social and psychological functioning also require knowledge of statistical methods for ascertaining reliability and validity. When your data analysis is complex, you would be well-advised to employ a statistical consultant.

Report the Results

Writing the report of your survey results requires communication skills, including the ability to write clearly and to present data in the form of tables and figures. To make oral presentations of your results, you need the ability to speak well in public and to prepare visual aids. It helps to have outside reviewers critique your initial report; you should plan to allow time for both the critiques and any subsequent revisions. If you print and disseminate many copies of your report, the associated expenses can be significant.

TIME, SCOPE, AND QUALITY

Ideally, surveyors prefer to make their own estimates of the amount of time needed to complete their surveys. Unfortunately, most surveys have due dates that the surveyors must respect.

The amount of time available for your survey will be a key factor in the survey's size, scope, quality, and costs. Time constraints limit your hiring choices to those people who can complete the survey tasks within the allotted periods, place boundaries on the survey's design and implementation, may affect the survey's quality, and are one determinant of the survey's costs. Example 7.5 compares two surveys to show the links among time, scope, quality, and costs.

EXAMPLE 7.5
Connections Among Time, Scope, Quality, and Costs in Surveys

Six elementary schools have joined together as a consortium to sponsor a survey to find out why young children start smoking. Among the questions the survey is to answer are these: Do children smoke because their friends do? Do parents smoke and thus serve as a negative model of adult behavior? How influential is advertising? What types of programs, events, or activities are most likely to be effective in teaching young children about the dangers of smoking?

The Consortium Board meets every 6 months. The board plans to use the survey's results as a basis for determining whether an antismoking program should be undertaken and, if so, what format it might take.

Example 7.5 continued

Case Study 1

The Consortium Board gives approval for the survey at its September meeting and requires that findings be presented within 6 months, in time for the board's next meeting in March. The survey team's schedule looks like this:

Month 1: Identify objectives and previously used surveys. Conduct a review of the published literature to assist in identifying reasonable aims for the survey. The literature will be used also in helping to locate other surveys that might be appropriate for use in the present survey (6 months is considered too short a time to develop and properly pilot-test an entirely new instrument).

Months 1 and 2: Ensure that the sample is readily attainable. The survey team plans to compile a list of families of children in all six schools and make sure that the addresses are current. All children will be included in the survey.

Months 2 and 3: Prepare, pilot-test, and revise the survey.

Month 4: Mail the survey and follow up when necessary.

Month 5: Clean, enter, and analyze the data.

Month 6: Write the report and prepare an oral presentation.

Comments: The survey team must hire an experienced reviewer because the literature on children and smoking is voluminous; an individual needs sophisticated skills to identify and select efficiently the highest-quality, most-relevant articles and instruments. It costs more to hire a skilled literature reviewer than it would cost to hire an unskilled one and then train and supervise him or her. The relatively short time line prevents the team

Example 7.5 continued

from targeting the survey directly to its own specific population and, with just 1 month for cleaning, entering, and analyzing the data and preparing a written and oral report, the team needs to hire experienced, skilled (and relatively costly) individuals.

Also, unless items and instruments that are demonstrably applicable (e.g., the same issues are covered in the appropriate language level) are found to be available, the survey's quality will be compromised.

Case Study 2

The Consortium Board gives approval for the survey at its September meeting and requires that findings be presented within 1 year, in time for the next September meeting. This is what the survey team plans:

Month 1: Identify the survey's objectives. Conduct a literature review and focus groups. Use the focus groups to target the survey's objectives and to determine if the survey should be an interview or a questionnaire.

Month 2: Design the survey. Ensure that the sample list is up-to-date and that all children are included on the list.

Month 3: Prepare the survey instrument.

Month 4: Pretest and pilot-test the instrument.

Month 5: Revise the instrument and have it reviewed.

Month 6: Administer the survey and conduct follow-ups.

Month 7: Enter and clean the data, and prepare the codebook.

Month 8: Analyze the data.

Month 9: Write the report.

Example 7.5 continued

Month 10: Have the report reviewed.

Month 11: Revise the report.

Month 12: Prepare the final written report and oral presentation.

Comments: The longer time line in this case permits the addition of a focus group for identifying the survey's objectives, a review of the sampling list for accuracy, reviews of the report, and preparation of a codebook. There is no guarantee that the longer time line will produce a better and more valid survey than the shorter time line. The longer time line is likely to cost more because of the longer length of employment for the team and the additional activities.

SURVEY BUDGETS

How much does a survey cost? This is a two-edged question. A quick answer is that a survey costs exactly the amount of money that has been allocated for it. This can range from $100 to the millions of dollars allocated for the U.S. Census. If you have $5,000 to conduct a survey, well, that is what you have. The only issue is whether you can conduct a survey that you believe will have valid findings given the amount of money you have to spend.

Another answer to the question regarding the cost of a survey is related to an ideal, or the amount of money and time you need to do a first-rate job. As a surveyor, you are likely to encounter both situations: (a) The price is "set," and (b) you set the price. Only experience can really tell you if 10 or 15 days is enough time to finish task X and whether person Y is worth the price you are required to pay.

The next few examples are based on the assumption that when you are asked to prepare a budget, you are left to your own devices (common enough in government and foundation funding and in business applications, just to name two situations you may encounter). Being left on your own, however, does not mean that you can plan for a survey that is as expensive as you think you need it to be. On the contrary, everyone loves a bargain. Whatever the cost of your survey study, you must be prepared to justify your budget, often in written form. Will 10 days be enough of Jones's time, for example? Is Jones worth $500 per hour? To justify spending the money for Jones's time, you will have to demonstrate that he or she is an experienced, even genius, survey developer who is definitely able to complete the task within the time allotted.

Costs of a Survey: A Checklist

✓ **Learn about direct costs.** These are all the expenses you will incur *because* of the survey. These include all salaries and benefits, supplies, travel, equipment, and so on.

✓ **Decide on the number of days (or hours) that constitute a working year.** Commonly used numbers are 230 days (1,840 hours) and 260 days (2,080

---

hours). You will use these numbers to show the proportion of time or "level of effort" given by each staff member.

Example: A person who spends 20% of his or her time on the project (assuming 260 days per year) is spending .20 × 260, or 52 days or 416 hours.

✓ Formulate survey tasks or activities in terms of the number of months it will take to complete each.

Example: Prepare survey instrument during Months 5 and 6.

✓ Estimate how long, in number of days (or hours), you will need each person to complete his or her assigned task.

Example: Jones, 10 days; Smith, 8 days. If required, convert the days into hours and compute an hourly rate (e.g., Jones: 10 days, or 80 hours).

✓ Learn the daily (and hourly) rate each person will need to be paid.

Example: Jones, $320 per day, or $40 per hour; Smith, $200 per day, or $25 per hour.

✓ Learn the costs of benefits (e.g., vacation, pension, and health)—usually a percentage of salaries. Sometimes benefits are called *labor overhead*.

Example: Benefits are 25% of Jones's salary. For example, the cost of benefits for 10 days of Jones's time is 10 × 320 per day × .25, or $800.

✓ Learn the costs of other expenses that will be incurred specifically for *this* survey.

Example: One 2-hour focus group with 10 participants costs $650. Each participant gets a $25 hono-

Costs of a Survey: A Checklist Continued

rarium, for a total of $250; refreshments cost $50; a focus group expert facilitator costs $300; the materials costs $50 for reproduction, notebooks, name tags, and so on.

✓ **Learn the indirect costs, or the costs that will be incurred to keep the survey team going.** Every individual and institution has indirect costs, sometimes called *overhead* or *general and administrative* (G&A) costs. Indirect costs are sometimes a prescribed percentage of the total cost of the survey (e.g., 10%).

Example: All routine "costs of doing business," such as workers' compensation and other insurance; attorney's and license fees; lights, rent, and supplies, such as paper and computer disks.

✓ If the survey lasts more than 1 year, build in cost-of-living increases.

✓ In for-profit consultation and contracting, you may be able to include a "fee." The fee is usually a percentage of the entire cost of the project and may range from about 3% to 10%.

✓ Be prepared to justify all costs in writing.

Example: The purchases include $200 for 2,000 labels (2 per student interviewed) @ .10 per label and $486 for one copy of MIRACLE software for the data management program.

To calculate the total cost of a survey, you must specify all of the survey's activities and tasks, when each activity is to be completed, who will be involved in completing each task, how many days each person will spend on each task, and the cost per hour for each staff person, as well as other direct costs and indirect costs. The checklist below can guide you in calculating costs and preparing a budget for your survey. The discussion that follows addresses how you can put each of the items on the checklist into practice.

Direct Costs: Salaries

First, you need to determine the survey tasks to be undertaken, the number of months it will take to complete the survey, and number of days available for each task. Suppose the Consortium Board in Example 7.5 asks the survey team to plan and prepare a 12-month budget for its Stop Smoking Survey. The team—which consists of Beth Jones, Yuki Smith, and Marvin Lee—begins the budget preparation process by preparing a table (see Example 7.6) that contains descriptions of the tasks to be accomplished, the months during which the tasks will be performed and completed, and the numbers of days the staff will need to complete each task. This table enables the survey team to tell quickly how long each task will take and how much staff time will be used. For example, 35 days of staff time will be needed to prepare the final report and oral presentation. Soon, the days of staff time will be converted into costs. Obviously, it is costlier to use many days of staff time than it is to use fewer days.

When you are preparing a budget, it is essential that you lay out all the relevant information in a table such as the one in Example 7.6. Doing so will help you to decide where you might trim the budget if you need to. For example, do Smith and Jones really need to spend 10 days each on the preparation of the final report and oral presentation? What will Lee

(text continues on page 136)

EXAMPLE 7.6
Tasks, Months, and Staff Days

Task	Month	Staff Members	Number of Days Spent by Each Staff Member on Task	Total Number of Days for All Members to Complete Task
Identify objectives; conduct literature review	1	Smith	20	35
		Jones	10	
		Lee	5	
Identify objectives; organize and conduct focus groups	1	Jones	10	15
		Lee	5	
Design the survey	2	Lee	15	20
		Smith	5	
Prepare the survey	3	Lee	20	45
		Jones	10	
		Smith	15	
Prepare packet for institutional review board	3-4	Jones	5	5
Pretest and pilot-test the instrument	4	Lee	15	35
		Jones	10	
		Smith	10	
Revise the instrument	5	Lee	10	15
		Smith	5	

Example 7.6 continued

Task	Month	Staff Members	Number of Days Spent by Each Staff Member on Task	Total Number of Days for All Members to Complete Task
Administer the survey	6	Lee	10	20
		Smith	10	
Enter and clean data; prepare the codebook	7	Lee	10	28
		Smith	3	
		Jones	15	
Analyze the data	8	Lee	15	30
		Jones	15	
Write the report	9	Lee	15	25
		Smith	5	
		Jones	5	
Have the report reviewed	10	Lee	5	5
Revise the report	11	Lee	10	10
Prepare the final report	12	Lee	15	35
		Smith	10	
		Jones	10	
Prepare the oral presentation	12	Lee	5	15
		Smith	5	
		Jones	5	

be doing during the 5 days the report is being reviewed in Month 10? Preparing such a table will also allow you to see clearly how much time each person is going to need for the particular project. For example, Marvin Lee will be working 155 days on the Stop Smoking Survey. Assuming 260 days is 1 working year, Marvin will be spending nearly 60%, or two-thirds, of his time on this project. If Marvin also has other projects and very limited time, you may want to ask, "Where can we trim Marvin's time and still get the job done?"

EXAMPLE 7.7
Additional Resources Needed for the Stop Smoking Survey

Task	Special Resources
Review literature	Reproduction of reports and surveys; reproduction of forms for abstracting content of literature; reference manager software
Conduct focus groups	Honoraria for participants; refreshments; notebooks for participants' materials
Design the survey	Staff (e.g., a research assistant) to review accuracy of addresses in database and follow up incorrect ones
Prepare IRB materials	Postage for one original and one follow-up mailing; printing costs for questionnaire
Administer the survey	Reproduction of materials (10 hard copies required)
Enter the data	Trained data enterer
Analyze the data	Programmer; statistician
Prepare reports	Paper for multiple copies of the report; graphics specialists for written and oral reports

Direct Costs: Resources

Practically all survey studies require personnel to provide administrative support. These persons may also receive benefits if they are employed for a certain percentage of time (for example, three-quarter-time employees may receive benefits, whereas one-quarter-time employees may not). Expenses for secretarial and clerical support are sometimes (but not always) considered direct costs. You also need to identify any special resources needed for your particular survey. A potential list of additional resources needed for the Stop Smoking Survey to find out about children and smoking appears in Example 7.7.

EXAMPLE 7.8
Contents of a Budget for Activities, Staff, and Entire Survey

This is a budget for a 1-year mail survey.

Budget Contents for an Activity: Prepare Final Report

Direct costs	Cost	Total

Survey personnel
    Marvin Lee—15 days
    Beth Jones—10 days
    Yuki Smith—10 days
    Research assistant support—15 days
      Personnel subtotal

Benefits (percentage of the subtotal)
    Marvin Lee
    Beth Jones
    Yuki Smith
      Benefits subtotal

Other direct costs
    Consultant: Statistician

Example 7.8 continued

Purchases: MIRACLE software
Other direct costs subtotal

Indirect costs
10% of direct costs

TOTAL BUDGET FOR ACTIVITY:

Budget Contents for Staff: Marvin Lee

Direct costs	Cost	Total
Days spent on survey: 155		
Salary per day		

Indirect costs
Benefits

TOTAL FOR MARVIN LEE:

Total Budget

Direct costs	Cost	Total

Survey personnel
Marvin Lee—155 days
Beth Jones—95 days
Yuki Smith—88 days
Research assistant support—165 days
Personnel subtotal

Indirect costs

Benefits (percentage of the subtotal)
Marvin Lee
Beth Jones
Yuki Smith
Research assistant
Benefits subtotal

Example 7.8 continued

Other direct costs
Consultants:
Graphics artist: To be named
ABC Data Entry, Inc.
John Becke, Programmer
Edward Parker, Statistician
Purchases: MIRACLE software
Paper
Reproduction of reports, surveys, and forms
Honoraria
Postage for survey mailings
Printing
    Other direct costs subtotal

Indirect costs
    10% of direct costs
        TOTAL BUDGET:

Budgets can be prepared for specific activities, individual staff members, and the entire survey. In Example 7.8, the items that are usually included in survey budgets are laid out in a general format typical of the kind used to record budgetary information. (The example includes none of the associated monetary figures because these vary so much from place to place and over time that any figures that might be included here would likely be completely irrelevant your own budget.) If you have all the needed information, you should have no trouble translating your budget items from this particular format to another.

BUDGET JUSTIFICATION

Budgets are often accompanied by justification of any or all of the following: choice of personnel, amount of time individuals are to spend on tasks or on the project, salaries, other direct costs, indirect costs, and any fees or purchases of

Guidelines for Reducing Survey Costs

- Shorten the duration of data collection.

- Reduce the number of follow-ups.

- Limit pilot testing to fewer respondents. (If you pilot-test 10 or more in a federally funded survey, you will need to get "clearance"—permission to proceed—from the appropriate federal agency. Having 9 or fewer participants in your pilot test also saves time and money.)

- Shorten instrument preparation time by adapting items and ideas from other surveys.

- Keep the instrument brief to reduce interviewer and respondent time.

- Use nonfinancial incentives, such as certificates of appreciation, to reward respondents.

- Use less expensive staff for day-to-day activities.

- Save your use of expensive staff for consultation and leadership.

- Comparison shop for all supplies and equipment.

- Reduce the number of activities.

- Shorten the amount of time each activity takes.

---

equipment and supplies. Example 7.9 displays some samples of budget justifications for staff, focus groups, and purchase of software.

HOW TO REDUCE COSTS

One of the most difficult aspects of budget preparation is usually performed after the bottom line—the total—is calcu-

EXAMPLE 7.9
Budget Justification

Staff

Marvin Lee will be the leader of the survey team and spend 155 days (or 63%) of his professional time on the project. Dr. Lee has conducted local and national surveys, the most recent of which is the Elementary School Behavior Questionnaire (ESB). For the ESB, he successfully performed many of the tasks required in the present study, including the conduct of literature reviews and focus groups and survey design, sampling, instrument preparation, data analysis, and report writing. He has worked as a surveyor for this institution for 10 years. His salary is based on his experience and education and is consistent with the salary schedule described in our handbook (which is on file).

Focus Group

A focus group is planned to assist in determining the objectives of the survey. We are aiming for 10 participants: 3 children, 2 parents, 2 teachers, 1 health professional, and 2 school administrators. Each will get an honorarium of $XX for a total of $XXX. Each participant will have a specially designed notebook with materials for discussion. Each notebook will cost $XX to produce, and 10 will cost $XXX. Light refreshments include cookies and soft drinks at $X per person, for a total of $XX.

Software

MIRACLE is a qualitative data management program. Comparison shopping (estimates upon request) found the least expensive price to be $XX.

lated for the first time. Usually, survey teams include in their initial budgets everything they think they will need—and probably then some. Invariably, budgets need trimming. You may be able to reduce the cost of your survey by applying the following guidelines.

Exercises

1. List three sources of survey objectives.

2. Make this question more concrete:

    How would you describe your health?

3. Rewrite these questions so that they are more appropriate for a survey.

    a. Age?

    b. How tall are you?

4. Name the type of sampling used in each of the following examples:

    Example A: The school has an alphabetical list of 300 students, 60 of whom will be asked to participate in a new reading program. The surveyor tosses a die and comes up with the number 3. Starting with the 3rd name on the list and continuing with the 8th, 13th, and so on, she continues sampling until she has 60 names.

Example B: Four of the schools are assigned to the experimental group and three to the control group.

Example C: The teachers are asked to give the survey to 10 colleagues.

5. Name four types of survey instruments.

6. Tell whether each of the following statements is true or false.

   a. A reliable survey is one that is relatively free of measurement error.

   b. A reliable survey is nearly always valid.

   c. Test-retest reliability is sometimes called internal consistency reliability.

   d. New Survey A, a measure of self-esteem, has content validity when people who score well on it also score well on Survey B, an older and valid measure of self-esteem.

   e. *Construct validity* is an appropriate term for a measure of hostility that accurately discriminates between hostile and nonhostile persons.

7. Tell whether you must consider or can ignore each of the following in choosing a method of analyzing survey data.

	1. Must Be Considered	2. Can Be Ignored
a. Whether data are nominal, ordinal, or numerical	1	2
b. Reliability of data collection	1	2
c. Validity of data collection	1	2
d. Assumptions of the analysis method	1	2
e. Validity of the research design	1	2
f. Whether the survey is an interview or self-administered questionnaire	1	2

8. What are eight main survey tasks?

9. List 12 questions to ask when pilot-testing mail and other self-administered questionnaires.

10. List 10 questions to ask when pilot-testing telephone interviews.

11. List 8 questions to ask when pilot-testing face-to-face interviews.

Suppose that you have been asked to create an informed consent form for a mail survey aimed at finding out about the health of South Asians in the United States. You are in charge of conducting the survey. You have purchased a list of South Asian family names from a company that you found on the Internet.

Your survey's objective is to determine the health status of South Asians in the United States. To facilitate your participants' returning the survey questionnaires, you plan to provide them with postage-paid, preaddressed envelopes. The survey takes approximately 20 minutes to complete. You are aware that this amount of time may cause some inconvenience for participants. Also, some of the questions are personal and may cause some discomfort. However, you believe that your survey's questions may help participants gain a better understanding of their own health, and that it is possible that the community will benefit because doctors may acquire new knowledge of the health care needs of South Asians. If the results of your study are disseminated, they may influence how much money will be spent on the health care needs of South Asians in the future. You plan to give each participant five dollars as a token of appreciation for the time he or she is taking and to help make up for any discomfort that may result from participation.

You plan to keep confidential all information obtained in connection with the survey; you will disclose data only with your participants' permission or as required by law. No names will be entered into any files or computer programs. All surveys will be destroyed at the end of the study. Your institution insists that participation must be voluntary and that participants can withdraw at any time without consequences of any kind. Participants may also refuse to answer any questions they don't want to answer and still remain in the study. You intend to place your name, address, phone number, and e-mail address on the form, so that potential respondents can get in touch with you.

Use the following headings to design your informed consent form:

Purpose of the study

Procedures

Potential risks and discomforts

Potential benefits to subjects and/or to society

Payment for participation

Confidentiality

Participation and withdrawal

Identification of investigators

ANSWERS

1. The literature, defined needs, and experts

2. In the past month, how often have you felt ill?

3. a. What is your birth date?

   OR How old were you on your last birthday?
   _____ years old

   b. How tall are you in inches?
   _____ inches

4. *Example A:* Systematic sampling
   Example B: Cluster sampling
   Example C: Snowball sampling

5. a. Interviews (telephone and in-person)

    b. Self-administered questionnaires (mail, computer-assisted, group)

    c. Observations

       Reviews of archives (notes, records)

6. a. True

    b. False

    c. False

    d. False

    e. True

7. a. Must be considered

    b. Must be considered

    c. Must be considered

    d. Must be considered

    e. Must be considered

    f. Can be ignored

8. Identify survey objectives, design the survey, prepare the survey instrument, pilot-test the instrument, administer the survey, organize the data, analyze the data, report the results

9. *Mail and other self-administered questionnaires*

    1. Are instructions for completing the survey clearly written?

    2. Are questions easy to understand?

    3. Do respondents know how to indicate responses (e.g., circle or mark the response; use a special pencil; use the space bar)?

4. Are the response choices mutually exclusive?

5. Are the response choices exhaustive?

6. If a mail questionnaire, do respondents understand what to do with completed questionnaires (e.g., return them by mail in a self-addressed envelope; fax them)?

7. If a mail questionnaire, do respondents understand when to return the completed survey?

8. If a computer-assisted survey, can respondents correctly use the commands?

9. If a computer-assisted survey, do respondents know how to change (or "correct") their answers?

10. If an incentive is given for completing the survey, do respondents understand how to obtain it (e.g., it will automatically be sent on receipt of completed survey; it is included with the questionnaire)?

11. Is the participants' privacy respected and protected?

12. Do respondents have any suggestions regarding the addition or deletion of questions, the clarification of instructions, or improvements in format?

10. *Telephone interviews*

1. Do interviewers understand how to ask questions and present options for responses?

2. Do interviewers know how to get in-depth information, when appropriate, by probing respondents' brief answers?

3. Do interviewers know how to record information?

4. Do interviewers know how to keep the interview to the agreed-on time limit?

5. Do interviewers know how to return completed interviews?

6. Are interviewers able to select the sample using the agreed-on instructions?

7. Can interviewers readily use the phone logs to record the number of times and when potential respondents were contacted?

8. Do interviewees understand the questions?

9. Do interviewees understand how to answer the questions (e.g., pick the top two; rate items according to whether they agree or disagree)?

10. Do interviewees agree that their privacy has been protected and respected?

11. *In-person interviews*

1. Do interviewers understand how to ask questions and present options for responses?

2. Do interviewers know how to get in-depth information, when appropriate, by probing respondents' brief answers?

3. Do interviewers know how to record information?

4. Do interviewers know how to keep the interview to the agreed-on time limit?

5. Do interviewers know how to return completed interviews?

6. Do interviewees understand the questions?

7. Do interviewees understand how to answer the questions (e.g., pick the top two; rate items according to whether they agree or disagree)?

8. Do interviewees agree that their privacy has been protected and respected?

Informed Consent Form

Title of Study:
South Asian Health and Use of Medical Services

We are asking you to participate in a research study conducted by AAAA from the Department of BBB. You were selected as a possible participant in this study because you have a South Asian family name.

- PURPOSE OF THE STUDY

    The purpose of this study is to determine the health status of South Asians and investigate what types of medical care they are receiving.

- PROCEDURES

    If you volunteer to participate in this study, we would ask you to fill out the enclosed survey, which asks questions about your health and medical care. Return the survey in the postage-paid envelope provided.

- POTENTIAL RISKS AND DISCOMFORTS

    This survey will take approximately 20 minutes. This may pose some inconvenience. Also, some questions are personal in nature. If you do not wish to answer these questions, you may leave them blank.

- POTENTIAL BENEFITS TO SUBJECTS
  AND/OR TO SOCIETY

    You may gain a better understanding of your own health by answering this survey. Your community will benefit because doctors will understand the health care needs of South Asians. The study may also influence how much money will be spent on the health care needs of South Asians in the future.

- PAYMENT FOR PARTICIPATION

  We are enclosing $5 for you. Please keep this money as our gift even if you do not wish to fill out the survey.

- CONFIDENTIALITY

  Any information that is obtained in connection with this study and that can be identified with you will remain confidential and will be disclosed only with your permission or as required by law. Your name will never be entered into any files or computer programs. All surveys will be destroyed at the end of the study.

- PARTICIPATION AND WITHDRAWAL

  You can choose whether to be in this study or not. If you volunteer to be in this study, you may withdraw at any time without consequences of any kind. You may also refuse to answer any questions you don't want to answer and still remain in the study. The investigators may withdraw you from this research if circumstances arise that warrant their doing so.

- IDENTIFICATION OF INVESTIGATORS

  If you have any questions or concerns about the research, please feel free to contact AAAA at (BBB) CCC-DDDO or EEE@hotstuffe.net. The mailing address is XXX Any Street, Any Town, State 9XXXX.

Suggested Readings

Afifi, A. A., & Clark, V. (1990). *Computer-aided multivariate analysis.* New York: Van Nostrand Reinhold.

Textbook on multivariate analysis with a practical approach. Discusses data entry, data screening, data reduction, and data analysis.

American Psychological Association. (1985). *Standards for educational and psychological testing.* Washington, DC: Author.

Classic work on reliability and validity and the standards that testers should achieve to ensure accuracy.

Babbie, E. (1990). *Survey research methods.* Belmont, CA: Wadsworth.

Fundamental reference on how to conduct survey research. Good examples of survey questions with accompanying rules for asking questions.

Baker, T. L. (1988). *Doing social research.* New York: McGraw-Hill.

A "how-to," with examples.

Bernard, H. R. (2000). *Social research methods: Qualitative and quantitative approaches.* Thousand Oaks, CA: Sage.

Great overview of social research methods; offers a little bit of everything, including much of interest to survey researchers.

Bradburn, N. M., & Sudman, S. (1992). The current status of questionnaire design. In P. N. Biemer, R. M. Groves, L. E. Lyberg, N. A. Mathiowetz, & S. Sudman (Eds.), *Measurement errors in surveys* (pp. 29-40). New York: John Wiley.

Addresses many of the major issues regarding questionnaire design and how to ask questions.

Braitman, L. (1991). Confidence intervals assess both clinical and statistical significance. *Annals of Internal Medicine, 114,* 515-517.

Contains one of the clearest explanations anywhere of the use of confidence intervals; highly recommended.

Brett, A., & Grodin, M. (1991). Ethical aspects of human experimentation in health services research. *Journal of the American Medical Association, 265,* 1854-1857.

Extremely important article because of its implications for experimental designs. The "participants" in experiments and their surveys are human, so the requirements of informed consent apply, as do such concepts as respect for privacy.

Campbell, D. T., & Stanley, J. C. (1963). *Experimental and quasi-experimental designs for research.* Chicago: Rand McNally.

Classic book on differing research designs. Describes threats to internal and external validity in detail and presents important discussion of issues pertaining to generalizability and how to get at "truth."

Cohen, S. B., & Machlin, S. R. (2000). Survey attrition considerations in the Medical Expenditure Panel Survey. *Journal of Economic and Social Measurement, 26,* 83-98.

One of three articles in this issue of the Journal of Economic and Social Measurement on methods of improving the accuracy and quality of health care surveys. Discusses nonresponse. Available on the Web site of the Agency for Healthcare Research and Quality (AHRQ; www.ahrq.gov). The Medical Expenditure Panel Survey (MEPS), sponsored by the AHRQ, was designed to produce national and regional estimates of health care use, expenditures, sources of payment, and insurance coverage of the U.S. population. (See also the entries in this list for Cohen & Yu, 2000; Winglee, Valliant, Brick, & Machlin, 2000.)

Cohen, S. B., & Yu, W. W. (2000). The impact of alternative sample allocation schemes on the precision of survey estimates derived from the National Medical Expenditure Panel Survey. *Journal of Economic and Social Measurement, 26,* 111-128.

One of three articles in this issue of the Journal of Economic and Social Measurement on methods of improving the accuracy and quality of health care surveys. Available on the Web site of the Agency for Healthcare Research and Quality (www.ahrq.gov). (See also the entries in this list for Cohen & Machlin, 2000; Winglee, Valliant, Brick, & Machlin, 2000.)

Converse, J. M., & Presser, S. (1986). *Survey questions: Handcrafting the standardized questionnaire.* Beverly Hills, CA: Sage.

Much of what you need to know on how to put a standardized questionnaire together.

Cook, D. C., & Campbell, D. T. (1979). *Quasi-experimentation: Design and analysis issues for field settings.* Boston: Houghton Mifflin.

Discusses the issues that arise in fieldwork and quasi-experimentation. Helps bring together issues that link design, sampling, and analysis.

Dawson, B., & Trapp, R. G. (2000). *Basic and clinical biostatistics* (3rd ed.). New York: McGraw-Hill.

Basic and essential primer on the use of statistics in medicine and medical care settings. Explains study designs and how to summarize and present data; discusses sampling and the main statistical methods used in analyzing data.

Dillman, D. A. (1978). *Mail and telephone surveys: The total design method.* New York: John Wiley.

Reviews the special issues associated with mail and telephone surveys.

Fink, A. (1993). *Evaluation fundamentals: Guiding health programs, research, and policy.* Newbury Park, CA: Sage.

Discusses survey design, sampling, analysis, and reporting from the point of view of program evaluators, whose work requires many of the same skills needed by survey researchers.

Fink, A., & Kosecoff, J. (1998). *How to conduct surveys: A step-by-step guide* (2nd ed.). Thousand Oaks, CA: Sage.

Gives many examples of survey questions and contains rules and guidelines for asking questions.

Frey, J. H. (1989). *Survey research by telephone.* Newbury Park, CA: Sage.

Gives excellent examples of questions and how to get needed information through telephone surveys.

Hambleton, R. K., & Zaal, J. N. (Eds.). (1991). *Advances in educational and psychological testing.* Boston: Kluwer Academic.

Important source of information on the concepts of reliability and validity in education and psychology.

Henry, G. T. (1990). *Practical sampling.* Newbury Park, CA: Sage.

Excellent source of information about sampling methods and sampling errors. Readers with knowledge of statistics will find this book most helpful, but it is worthwhile even for readers whose statistical knowledge is basic.

Kalton, G. (1983). *Introduction to survey sampling.* Beverly Hills, CA: Sage.

Excellent discussion of survey sampling; requires at least some understanding of statistics.

Kish, L. (1965). *Survey sampling.* New York: John Wiley.

A classic book; useful for resolving issues that arise during the implementation of sampling designs.

Kraemer, H. C., & Thiemann, S. (1987). *How many subjects? Statistical power analysis in research.* Newbury Park, CA: Sage.

Thorough discussion of the complexity of statistical power analysis; requires at least some understanding of statistics.

Mays, N., & Pope, C. (Eds.). (1999). *Qualitative research in health care* (2nd ed.). London: BMJ Books.

Available at www.bmjpg.com, where the full text of each of the chapters can also be viewed: "Qualitative Methods in Health Research," by Catherine Pope and Nicholas Mays; "Qualitative Interviews in Health Care Research," by Nicky Britten; "Focus Groups With Users and Providers of Health Care," by Jenny Kitzinger; "Observational Methods in Health Care Settings," by Catherine Pope and Nicholas Mays; "Using the Delphi and Nominal Group Technique in Health Services Research," by Jeremy Jones and Duncan Hunter; "Using Case Studies in Health Services and Policy Research," by Justin Keen and Tim Packwood; "Using Qualitative Methods in Health-Related Action Research," by Julienne Meyer; "Analysing Qualitative Data," by Catherine Pope, Sue Ziebland, and Nicholas Mays; and "Quality in Qualitative Health Research," by Nicholas Mays and Catherine Pope.

McDowell, I., & Newell, C. (1996). *Measuring health: A guide to rating scales and questionnaires* (2nd ed.). New York: Oxford University Press.

Provides numerous examples of health measurement techniques and scales available to the survey researcher interested in health. Also discusses the validity and reliability of important health measures.

Miller, D. C. (1991). *Handbook of research design and social measurement.* Newbury Park, CA: Sage.

Discusses and defines all possible components of social research. Includes selected sociometric scales and indexes and is a very good source of questions pertaining to social status, group structure, organizational structure, job satisfaction, community, family and marriage, and attitudes.

Morris, L. L., Fitz-Gibbon, C. T., & Lindheim, E. (1987). *Program evaluation kit, Vol. 7: How to measure performance and use tests* (2nd ed., J. L. Herman, Series Ed.). Newbury Park, CA: Sage.

Excellent discussion of reliability and validity as they apply to measurements of student performance.

Patton, M. Q. (1999). Enhancing the quality and credibility of qualitative analysis. In K. J. Devers, S. Sofaer, & T. G. Randall (Eds.), Qualitative methods in health services research [Special suppl.]. *Health Services Research, 34,* 1189-1208.

Pfeiffer, W. S. (1991). *Technical writing.* New York: Macmillan.

Provides useful tips on the details of putting together a formal report. Discusses the cover and title page, table of contents, and executive summary, and offers suggestions for preparing charts and giving oral presentations.

Pincus H. A., Lieberman J. A., & Ferris, S. (1999). *Ethics in psychiatric research: A resource manual for human subjects protection.* Washington, DC: American Psychiatric Association.

Superb resource; helpful for anyone in any field who needs to understand ethical issues in human subjects research. Contains The Belmont Report and Title 45, Part 46, of the U.S. Code of Federal Regulations, "Protection of Human Subjects."

Schuman, H., & Presser, S. (1981). *Questions and answers in attitude surveys.* New York: Academic Press.

Raises and addresses many important issues regarding how to design questions about attitudes; includes good examples.

Siegel, S. (1956). *Nonparametric statistics for the behavioral sciences.* New York: McGraw-Hill.

Classic textbook on nonparametric statistics.

Sofaer, S. (1999). Qualitative methods: What are they and why use them? In K. J. Devers, S. Sofaer, & T. G. Randall (Eds.), Qualitative methods in health services research [Special suppl.]. *Health Services Research, 34,* 1101-1118.

Sudman, S., & Bradburn, N. M. (1982). *Asking questions.* San Francisco: Jossey-Bass.

Very good source for examples of how to write questions pertaining to knowledge, attitudes, behavior, and demographics.

U.S. Department of Health and Human Services, Office of Human Research Protections. Web site: ohrp.osophs.dhhs.gov

Internet site for information on and publications of the U.S. Office of Human Research Protections.

Winglee, M., Valliant, R., Brick, J. M., & Machlin, S. R. (2000). Probability matching of medical events. *Journal of Economic and Social Measurement, 26,* 129-140.

One of three articles in this issue of the Journal of Economic and Social Measurement on methods of improving the accuracy and quality of health care surveys. Reports on the difficulties of matching based on reports of medical care use and expenditures. Available on the Web site of the Agency for Healthcare Research and Quality (www.ahrq.gov). (See also the entries in this list for Cohen & Machlin, 2000; Cohen & Yu, 2000.)

Glossary

Belmont Report—Shortened title of *The Belmont Report: Ethical Principles and Guidelines for the Protection of Human Subjects of Research,* which was prepared by the National Commission for the Protection of Human Subjects of Biomedical and Behavioral Research in 1979. It is still regarded as the foundation of ethical research, including survey research.

Case controls—Control groups formed from retrospective surveys of previous study findings. For example, a study comparing survey findings from a new sample of smokers and nonsmokers to a survey of the past medical records of a sample of smokers and nonsmokers of the same age, health, and socioeconomic status uses a case-control design.

Categorical (or nominal) response choices—Response choices that have no numerical or preferential values. For example, when respondents answer a question regarding their sex or gender, they simply name themselves as belonging to one of two categories: male or female.

Closed question (or closed-ended question)—A question for which the respondent is provided preselected answers to choose among (see **open-ended question**).

Cluster—A naturally occurring unit (e.g., a school or university, which has many classrooms, students, and teachers; a hospital; or a metropolitan statistical area).

Cohort design—A study design concerned with a particular cohort, or group. Cohort designs can be retrospective, or look back over time (a historical cohort), if the events being studied actually occurred before the onset of the surveys; they can also be forward-looking, or prospective, seeking data about changes in specific populations.

Concurrent controls—Control groups assembled at the same time as the experimental groups with which they are compared. For example, when 10 of 20 schools are randomly assigned to an experimental group and the other 10 are assigned to a control at the same time, the result is a randomized controlled trial or true experiment. When participants in concurrent control groups are not randomly assigned, the results are called non-randomized controlled trials, quasi-experiments, or nonequivalent controls.

Concurrent validity—The extent to which there is agreement on two assessments of a measure or a new measure is compared favorably with one that is already considered valid.

Construct validity—The extent to which a survey distinguishes between people who do and do not have certain characteristics. Construct validity is established experimentally.

Content analysis—A method for analyzing and interpreting qualitative survey data by examining the content of written or recorded documents and recorded observations of behavior.

Content validity—The extent to which a measure thoroughly and appropriately assesses the skills or characteristics it is intended to measure.

Convenience sample—A sample made up of individuals the researcher finds to be easily available and willing to participate.

Correlation—Estimation of the relationship between two or more variables.

Criterion validity—The extent to which a measure forecasts future performance (predictive validity) or compares favorably in its results with other, more well-established surveys (concurrent validity).

Cronbach's coefficient alpha—A statistical method of determining a survey's internal consistency; the average of all the correlations between each item and the total score.

Cross-sectional survey—A survey that provides descriptive data at one fixed point in time (e.g., a survey of American voters' current choices).

Dependent variables—The responses to, outcomes of, or results of interventions.

Descriptive designs (or observational designs)—Designs for surveys that produce information on groups and phenomena that already exist; no new groups are created in the survey study.

Equivalence (or alternate-form reliability)—The extent to which two items measure the same concepts at the same level of difficulty.

Experimental designs—Designs characterized by the comparison of two or more groups, at least one of which is experimental and the others of which are control (or comparison) groups.

Face validity—How a measure appears on the surface: Does it seem to ask all the needed questions?

Frequency count—A computation of how many people fit into a category (men or women, under or over 70 years of age, saw five or more movies last year or did not).

Historical controls—Control groups formed from data collected from participants in other surveys.

Inclusion criteria—The characteristics a person is required to have to be eligible for participation in the survey (exclusion criteria are those characteristics that rule out certain people).

Independent variables (or explanatory or predictor variables)—Variables used to explain or predict a response, outcome, or result (the dependent variable).

Informed consent—Consent given by subjects certifying that they are participating with full knowledge of the risks and benefits of participation, the activities that constitute participation, the terms of participation, and their rights as research subjects.

Institutional review board (IRB)—An administrative body whose purpose is to protect the rights and welfare of human subjects who are recruited to participate in research activities.

Internal consistency (or homogeneity)—The extent to which all items or questions assess the same skill, characteristic, or quality.

Interrater reliability—The extent to which two or more individual raters agree.

Intrarater reliability—A single rater's consistency of measurement.

Nonprobability sample—A sample for which there is no guarantee that all eligible units have an equal chance of being included. The main advantages of using nonprobability samples are that they are relatively convenient and economical to assemble, and they are appropriate for many surveys.

Numerical response choices—Response choices involving numbers; used for questions such as age (e.g., number of years) or height (e.g., number of meters).

Open-ended question (or open question)—A question that requires the respondent to use his or her own words in answering (see **closed question**).

Ordinal response choices—Response choices that respondents use to rate or order items, say, from very positive to very negative.

Pilot test—An initial test of the survey, well before it is made final. The pilot test is conducted with members of the target population and in the same setting as the actual survey.

Probability sampling—Sampling that provides a statistical basis for saying that a sample is representative of the study or target population.

Qualitative survey—A survey that concentrates on the meanings people attach to their experiences and on the ways they express themselves. A qualitative survey answers questions such as "What is X, and how do different people, communities, and cultures think and feel about X, and why?"

Quota sampling—Sampling in which the population being studied is divided into subgroups (such as male and female, younger and older) and the numbers of subgroup members in the sample are proportional to the numbers in the larger population.

Reliable survey instrument—An instrument that is relatively free of "measurement error." Measurement error occurs when individuals' obtained scores are different from their true scores, which can be obtained only from perfect measures. A reliable survey instrument yields consistent scores over time.

Representative sample—A sample in which important population characteristics (e.g., age, gender, health status) are distributed similarly to the way they are distributed in the population at large.

GLOSSARY

Researcher misconduct—Problematic behaviors on the part of researchers, whether intentional or not, that can distort survey findings; examples include fabrication or falsification of data and plagiarism.

Response rate—The number of persons who respond (numerator) divided by the number of eligible respondents (denominator).

Sample—A portion or subset of a larger group called a *population*. A good sample is a miniature version of the population of which it is a part; the best sample is representative of, or a model of, the population.

Sample size—The number of units that one needs to survey to get precise and reliable findings. The units can be people (e.g., men and women over and under 45 years of age), places (e.g., counties, hospitals, schools), or things (e.g., medical or school records).

Self-controls—Groups that serve as their own control groups through being surveyed at two different times. Studies using self-controls require premeasures and postmeasures and are called longitudinal, pretest-posttest, or before-after designs.

Simple random sampling—Sampling in which every subject or unit has an equal chance of being selected. Members of the target population are selected one at a time and independently. Once they have been selected, they are not eligible for a second chance and are not returned to the pool.

Snowball sampling—Sampling that relies on previously identified members of a group to identify other members of the population.

Statistical significance—The result achieved when observed differences are shown to occur at a level not explainable by chance.

Statistical survey—A survey that aims to answer quantitative questions such as, "How many Xs are there?" "What is the average X, and how does it compare to the average Y?"

Stratified random sampling—A sampling method in which the population is divided into subgroups, or "strata," and a sample is then randomly selected from each subgroup.

Structured observations—Observations made to collect data visually. In studies using structured observations, observers are guided in focusing on specific actions or characteristics.

Structured record review—A survey that uses a specially created form to guide the collection of data from financial, medical, school, and other records, including electronic, written, and filmed documents.

Survey—A system for collecting information from or about people in order to describe, compare, or explain their knowledge, attitudes, and behavior.

Test-retest reliability—An index of a survey's stability. A survey is stable if the correlation between scores from one time to another is high.

Triangulation—The collection of data from different sources (such as interviews and field notes) or different surveyors in different places, based on the assumption that if multiple sources of information produce similar results, the credibility of the survey's findings are enhanced.

Validity—The degree to which a survey instrument assesses what it purports to measure.

Variable—A measurable characteristic that varies in a population. For example, weight is a variable, and all persons weighing 55 kilograms have the same numerical weight. Satisfaction with a product is also a variable.

GLOSSARY

About the Author

Arlene Fink, Ph.D., is Professor of Medicine and Public Health at the University of California, Los Angeles. She is on the Policy Advisory Board of UCLA's Robert Wood Johnson Clinical Scholars Program, a consultant to the UCLA-Neuropsychiatric Institute Health Services Research Center, and President of Arlene Fink Associates, a research and evaluation company. She has conducted surveys and evaluations throughout the United States and abroad and has trained thousands of health professionals, social scientists, and educators in survey research, program evaluation, and outcomes and effectiveness research. Her published works include more than 100 articles, books, and monographs. She is co-author of *How to Conduct Surveys: A Step-by-Step Guide* and author of *Evaluation Fundamentals: Guiding Health Programs, Research, and Policy*; *Evaluation for Education and Psychology*; and *Conducting Research Literative Reviews: From Paper to the Internet.*